The Art of Coarse Office Life

C

Other books by Michael Green

The Coarse Series

The Art of Coarse Rugby
The Art of Coarse Sailing
Even Coarser Rugby
The Art of Coarse Sport
The Art of Coarse Acting
The Art of Coarse Golf
The Art of Coarse Moving (A Roof Over My Head)
The Art of Coarse Drinking
The Art of Coarse Cruising
Even Coarser Sport
The Art of Coarse Sex

Novels

Don't Print My Name Upside Down
Squire Haggard's Journal

Plays

Four Plays for Coarse Actors (Samuel French)
The Coarse Acting Show Two (Samuel French)
The Third Great Coarse Acting Show (Samuel French)

Others

Tonight Josephine (Secker and Warburg)
Don't Swing From the Balcony, Romeo (Secker and Warburg)
Michael Green's Rugby Alphabet (Pelham)
Stage Names and Effects (Herbert Jenkins)

The Art of
Coarse Office Life

or
'He's just popped out'

Michael Green
Illustrated by John Jensen

Century
London

Text © copyright Michael Green 1985
Illustrations © John Jensen 1985

First published in Great Britain in 1985 by
Century
An imprint of Century Hutchinson Ltd.
Chandos Place, London WC2

Printed and bound in Great Britain by
Anchor Brendon Ltd, Tiptree, Essex

British Library Cataloguing in Publication Data
Green, Michael, *1927–*
    The art of coarse office life, or, 'He's just
    popped out'.
    1. Office practice——Anecdotes, facetiae, satire,
    etc.
    I. Title
    651'.0207   HF5547.5

ISBN 0 7126 1062 6

Contents

5

Author's Note

Ever since somebody sank a yacht following my advice in *The Art of Coarse Sailing* (I think it was the bit about not being afraid of rocks), I have felt obliged to issue a warning that I am not responsible for any damage caused by using the so-called advice in my books, and that applies just as much this time. If a reader is sacked through following a tip recommended here, don't blame me. The warning is doubly necessary on this occasion, as a few paragraphs appeared in *The Art of Coarse Drinking*. I would not like anyone to be poisoned as well as fired.

Michael Green

CENTURY HUTCHINSON
LIMITED

Inter-Office Memo

From: Joanne
....

To: Editorial Director
....

Someone called Michael Bean rang and said he had forgotten to put a forward in The Art of Cursed Office Life. He said he wanted to thank the friends and colleagues who had helped him, sometimes without knowing it, and in particular a chap called Peter Hicks, whose lurid experiences in business were such an inspiration.

He said it was desperately urgent. I told him you'd just gone out. Let me know when you start taking calls again.

1

An Introduction to Coarse Office Life

So clear in his great office . . . .
Shakespeare, *Macbeth*

If anyone should ask my qualifications for writing a book with
this title I would retort that I have the finest qualification of all:
I was sacked from my first office job at the age of sixteen, and
not for some petty misdemeanour such as turning up late but
for a flamboyant gesture of defiance. Single-handed, I printed
a special edition of the local evening paper at midnight.
Unfortunately the management knew nothing about it until
they stumbled upon the wrecked machinery in the morning.

As a new recruit to the staff, with the somewhat dubious title
of editorial messenger, I had been working late with a young
colleague and we had to go out through the works exit. As we
passed through the half-lit machine room with its printing
presses my pal said, 'I wonder how these things work?'

'Easy,' I replied, having made friends with a machine
operator. 'You just switch on the mains over there and press the
button there.' We were silent for a moment, looking at each
other. These things are tempting when you're sixteen. 'Show
me,' he said. I swaggered over and switched on the mains; I
pressed the button. With a roar the great machines burst into
life and began spewing hundreds of yards of newsprint all over
the building. There is a mile of paper in a reel of newsprint. The
reel snapped under the strain and rolled on remorselessly,

sending its contents out like a flood which engulfed us. I had to struggle to the surface, arms waving like a drowning man.

It was a small, family firm and the elderly managing director sacked me personally.

'I wonder,' he said, 'if you have ever considered whether you are suitable for a career in an office? Perhaps something more active such as working in a garage would be more in your line. You obviously have a keen interest in machinery. Some people are better with their hands than their heads.'

Yet despite this warning I have spent the rest of my life in and out of offices. Like bars, they're unavoidable. Try to earn a living and you keep ending up in an office, either your own or somebody else's. Passing through so many over the years, I have watched fascinated at the workings of Coarse Office Life.

Perhaps I should explain the word 'Coarse' as used in the title. In this sense it has nothing to do with its normal meaning. As I have explained in the other 'Coarse' books, it does not mean something crude and unpleasant, such as eating mashed potatoes with your fingers or making rude noises at people you don't like. It is a lifestyle, but not so much a Coarse Person's attitude to life as life's attitude to him (or her). It is the way things get done in real life, as opposed to the lofty theoretical manner laid down by the authorities. Thus a Coarse Sailor is one who, in a crisis, can't help forgetting all that nautical stuff about port and starboard and shouts, 'For God's sake turn left, you fool!' Coarse Actors abound on the amateur stage, and they may be defined as people who know when to come on stage but not where (although there are several alternative definitions such as 'They always know the last play better than the one they're actually in'). That most demanding of all games, rugby football, has its Coarse segment also, far removed from the conventional image of fit young giants impervious to pain. Coarse rugby is a game played by fewer than fifteen a side, at least half of whom should be totally unfit, not merely for rugby but for anything else as well. Its practitioners may be seen

10

yelping round suburban playing fields on any Saturday after-noon when they aren't in the bar.

Here is a simple test by which the reader can judge whether he or she has any Coarseness in their everyday life:

1. Does the garage man call you 'sir' or 'madam'; or 'squire', 'chum', 'friend', 'lady', 'love' or 'you'?
2. Does he ever kick your car?
3. Does he advise you to take it somewhere else to have it repaired?
4. Do shop assistants go on talking to each other when you want serving?
5. When you cash a cheque at the bank, do they go away to see if there is any money in the account?
6. Is it always *you* who has to step off the pavement for other people?
7. Do bar staff look at you and then serve the person standing behind?

The same sort of questions can be applied to office life.

Coarse Office Quiz

1. Does the commissionaire call you 'sir' or 'madam'? Or 'Shorty', 'Nobby', 'Lanky', 'Curly' or 'Beautiful'?
2. Has he ever touched his cap and cried, 'Gawd bless you'?
3. Do the firm's female receptionists continue to file their nails while talking to you? (If she files *your* nails, see *The Art of Coarse Sex*.)
4. Do you have the key to the executive washroom? (If so, put it back before anyone finds out.)
5. When visiting another firm over lunch, do they say 'Come into the senior dining room'; 'The canteen's pretty good'; or 'The men usually go to the fish and chip shop'?
6. Do you have to share a toilet with anyone? (NB Not while actually using the cubicle, just as a general rule.)

11

Do female receptionists continue to file their nails while talking to you?

7. Has the receptionist ever reported your arrival by saying, 'There's a person downstairs who wants to see you'?

8. If someone spills something on the office floor, do you (a) abuse them (b) tell somebody to clean it up (c) ask somebody to clean it up (d) implore somebody to clean it up (e) clean it up yourself (f) go round and do a bit of general dusting as well (g) abjectly apologize to everybody for taking so long to clean it up?

9. Was lunch (a) smoked salmon and chicken supreme (b) shepherd's pie (c) a sandwich (d) three pints of bitter (e) a cigarette and a cough?

10. Did you (a) send your secretary out to buy this book (b) buy it yourself (c) borrow it from the library (d) pinch it off a colleague's desk?

11. Is the wife referred to as (a) your good lady (b) Mrs Jenkins (c) that woman?

12. When a company reorganization is announced, do you (a) shout: 'Yippee! Now we might get some efficiency,' (b) say: 'Mark my words, this obsession with change will get us nowhere,' (c) apply for redundancy (d) advertise for a job (e) flee the country?

13. If you find yourself at a bar with a member of senior management does he (a) buy you a drink (b) buy his own (c) ask you to buy him one (d) tell you to buy two drinks and put it on expenses (e) ignore you (f) leave (g) ask what the hell you are doing there?

14. (Women only): On your birthday does your boss give you (a) an expensive bottle of perfume (b) chocolates (c) a ballpoint pen with the company insignia?

15. (Women only): When members of the staff want to seduce you do they (a) buy you an expensive dinner (b) send flowers (c) take you out for half a pint of beer at the local pub and then say, 'All right, your place or mine?'?

16. (Men only): When you try to seduce a girl in the office does she say, (a) 'Oh, Mr Smith this is very sudden!' (b) 'I like you,

Charlie, but . . .' (c) 'Stop pawing me around, you dumb clot,' (d) start retching?

The answers should be self-evident. I would not expect any reader to have a 100 per cent failure rate but if so I advise them to seek help immediately, preferably not from me. I have problems, too.

So what is a definition of a Coarse Office Person? It's a horrid phrase, but the only one that expresses the true meaning. Henceforth, however, it will be abbreviated to COP on most occasions. One characteristic common to all COPs is that they never have everything they require, whether it's information, knowledge, qualifications, ambition or pencils. There is always one item missing. So a Coarse Office Person could be defined as one who, if they have to attend a conference, knows where it is and when it is, but not *why* it is. If they do know the reason for the conference, and when it is, they will have forgotten *where* it is. And if they know where and why it is, they won't know *when* it is. Thus it is perfectly possible for a COP to arrive at a conference late and start speaking on the wrong subject. Like an old friend who found himself giving a speech prepared for Swedish businessmen to a conference in Japan. It even contained Swedish jokes and puns. 'They were baffled, but polite,' he said.

That of course is only one facet of a COP. Another thing that distinguishes them is that they rarely have their own office; they have to share everything from rooms to computers. They are always on the move, too. You have to be quick to catch a COP as he flits by. That is how they survive. So it could be said a COP is someone who is either going to be back in a minute or has just gone out.

A further characteristic is that Coarse people are always on the brink of a disaster which somehow never occurs. If, as the poet says, 'Time's wingéd chariot' is hovering near for us all, a COP has got it standing outside the door blowing its horn. Yet

14

'They were baffled, but polite'

they are great survivors. Somehow the threatened calamity never happens or strikes somebody else.

Naturally, not everyone is a full-blooded COP. The world of business and government is not entirely staffed by accident-prone buffoons.* But everybody without exception has *something* of the Coarse Office about them, even those who have been promoted. Many a departmental head or product manager is still struggling with the job, such as the close friend who became managing director of a famous food company. 'Basically I'm still an accountant at heart,' he used to say, and he found the tough executive world rather too hot. His chief problem was he couldn't bring himself to sack anyone. In the end he had to hire a special man to sack people, but then he wanted to fire the sacker and found he couldn't do it because he liked him too much. So Coarse business stretches its tentacles to the highest level. We all have a touch of the COP, and even those at the top have passed through the Coarse world on the way up, although they would probably deny strenuously that they once used to help themselves from the boss's drinks cabinet.

In a world increasingly intolerant of human failings it is a great mistake to think that everybody else fits in better than oneself. That is not always so. A nervous, insecure heart beats beneath many a confident silk shirt. By describing and analysing the Coarse Office this book may help readers realize they are not alone in the Great Office Struggle, which is not so much a rat race as an endurance contest between mice.

* I think.

2

How Not to Communicate with People

Across the wires, the electric message came:
'He is no better, he is much the same.'
Alfred Austin

The essential purpose of an office is communication. Nothing is manufactured there; its only reason for existence is to receive and pass on information. It is unfortunate, therefore, that in most offices those employed spend a lot of time writing and talking to each other but failing to communicate. Most of the average working day in any office is taken up not with decision-making, innovating, organizing or anything constructive, but simply with trying to get through to other people.

There is only one certain way of contacting a person and that is to grab them by the coat, thrust your face against theirs, and speak loudly and distinctly. Even that will probably fail, since the shock of having to listen to a plain statement of fact delivered face-to-face will be too much for the listener. I once saw a distraught colleague, exhausted with failing to contact a man by phone and memo, pin him in his chair by thrusting a hand on his chest while he delivered what he wanted to say. It was quite simple, just a short message to the effect that he would like the copy of the annual report he'd been promised six days ago. But he totally failed to get through. When he'd finished, the other chap brushed himself down and said, 'I think you'd better put that in writing, old man.' It was one of the few occasions when I have actually seen someone turn

Trying to get through to other people

purple and claw the air. I thought they only did that in books.
The fact is, most people in Coarse Offices don't *want* to be
communicated with. That means work, worry or decisions.
They may go through the farce of surrounding themselves with
all the paraphernalia of communication, bleepers, bloobers,
radiophones, intercoms and so on, but this is all a blind. The
object of these is to prevent communication rather than aid it.
There is always safety in shielding behind electronic devices – it
avoids the dreaded face-to-face confrontation; it means you can
say you're tied up when you're reading the office copy of *Adult
Sex*. Law 35 of Coarse Office Life states: The more electronic
communicating devices employed, the less available a person
will be.

The greatest aid to non-communication is the good old-
fashioned telephone. Communication by phone between two
British business people is almost impossible. There will never
be a time when one of them is not in conference, at lunch, out of
the office, away today, busy at the moment, tied up just now,
seeing somebody, up at the Manchester office, coming in late
this morning, leaving early this afternoon, gone to the dentist,
had to see the doctor, got an appointment at the hospital, in
New York, on holiday, sick or on the other line.

In any case the times when senior staff can be found are few,
and even these brief moments are sometimes contracted. For
instance, senior officers in the armed forces cannot be traced
after 12.30 p.m. on Fridays, as their weekend begins then (if the
Russians attacked this country on a Friday afternoon they
would find it even more undefended than usual). There is a
tendency in the City of London for the weekend to commence at
Friday lunchtime and last until Monday midday ('I'm afraid
he's still on his way from Hampshire'). Elsewhere the weekend
may be more subtly disguised. A long, late lunch at some
remote outpost and then it's 'not worth returning to the office'.

As the stock phrases quoted previously are usually excuses,
do not be put off if the matter is urgent. It's surprising how

19

quickly they get off 'the other line' when told the bank manager is on the phone. A useful wheeze is to leave a vague message which suggests that the issue is important personally – 'Would you tell him I'm speaking from the bank?' or something similar. When called back, excuse yourself by saying, 'The silly girl got it wrong. I said nothing about a bank. I said the weather was rather dank.' Note that this wheeze contains Law 43 of Coarse Office Life: When you have failed to communicate, blame somebody else. The switchboard are good scapegoats and there are 'usually a few old scores to settle with them anyhow. Also, no one sees the switchboard people – they live in remote basements cut off from society, so there's no chance of having a row in the corridor. Don't feel guilty – they have their own ways of getting revenge, such as cutting you off in the middle of a vital call from Frankfurt.

However, the drama people put on when it is realized that the caller really ought to be put through would grace any West End theatre. After stone-walling with the usual 'He's at a meeting' the speaker suddenly says, 'Oh, just a minute, I think I hear him now.' What is actually happening is that she is waving to her boss and gesticulating at the mouthpiece, grimacing a silent message to the effect that this is one call he ought to take. I'm sure some secretaries and receptionists actually make up a little sort of radio play, tapping a pencil on the desk to imitate footsteps and holding an imaginary conversation, 'Hullo sir, nice to see you. Got back from your meeting most unexpectedly, didn't you? Mr Michael Green is on the phone. Yes, I know you're always pleased to talk to him, I'll put him through. . . .'

The most important thing to remember about the telephone is that you can still be heard when you put your hand over the mouthpiece to talk to someone else. I owe whatever success I've had in life to this simple realization, which came to me in 1968 when I telephoned a firm for which I did some freelance work, to complain my cheque hadn't arrived.

There was the inevitable 'Just a minute', and then that cottonwool feeling of a hand pressed over the phone. I listened hard. 'It's that stupid bastard Michael Green complaining we've not paid him again.' I could even hear the reply. 'He's lucky, he ought to pay us – the rotten work he does.'

'What shall I do?'

'Tell him to —— off.'

'No, seriously.'

'All right, tell him the cheque's in the post.'

'Is it?'

'How the hell do I know?'

A pause.

'Hello, Michael,' said a honeyed voice. 'Sorry to keep you waiting, but apparently your cheque was held up because the chief cashier was ill and there was nobody to sign it, ha, ha. But I'm assured it's winging it's way to you through the post at this very moment in time, old man. You should get it tomorrow or the day after at the latest. Is that all right? We like to keep you happy, you know. . . .'

More damage has been done to people's careers by the pathetic belief that the caller can't hear if you put a hand over the mouthpiece than by any other single agency. I remember the technical director of a firm telling me that, shortly after taking over, he rang up a department in his own company for some information without revealing who he was.

'I have a query about the XZ194A' he said. The reply came, 'Hold on, I'll find out who deals with it.' Then came the hand over the phone and a voice saying, 'Who's the expert on the XZ194A?' There was some muttering and someone was heard to shout across the room, 'You are.' A pause and then, 'Well, actually it appears that *I* am the expert on the XZ194A.'

In skilled hands the business letter can be rendered as useless as the telephone, and the two methods combined form an impenetrable wall of non-communication. The essence is to avoid the point entirely. Say a firm complains of delay in delivery. Nothing can be done about it, as the production department are incompetent, but a reply must be sent, so a typical answer might be:

International Desecration PLC

Desperation House,
London, W.1.

Dear Mr. Jones,

Thank you for your letter. We are sorry some supplies were not quite what you ordered but this is being rectified and I am assured your next batch will be entirely up to specification. Owing to the extension of our premises some departments have recently been placed in a non-operative posture situation.

Yours sincerely,

This letter not only avoids the issue but further clouds the scene with meaningless jargon at the end. The wretched Mr Jones, when he receives this gibberish with a headache one Monday morning, will simply groan and throw it away. Banks are particularly good at avoiding the issue when a customer complains, and anyone who wishes to master the art should study their letters as models.

Small firms and individuals are vulnerable to this sort of thing, as they haven't the staff to deal with protracted correspondence. The letter is picked off the wet doormat of a works on some windy industrial estate in South Wales, perhaps. The harrassed proprietor is without his sole office staff – she has gone to the doctor. The foreman has just insulted him and out of the window he can see a lorry driver urinating against the wheel of his vehicle, a sign that the drains are blocked again. The bank is pressing him for the £10,000 he borrowed; his mail consists largely of bills. At this moment he opens the letter. 'Sorry some supplies not quite what you ordered. . . .' Surely he wrote about delay in delivery? Or did he? 'Oh hell. I can't bother, I've got to pacify the foreman and see the bank manager and unblock the toilet. . . .' The matter is forgotten for a week, and a week is a long time in business.

A further refinement consists of writing an extremely long letter in the hope that the recipient will be exhausted before he gets to the end. The point of the letter is in the penultimate paragraph, which may never be read.

The ultimate in anti-communication is to write: 'Thank you for your letter, the contents of which have been noted.' I remember that reply being sent by a national newspaper to a poor man whose life had just been wrecked by their misreporting. It is a reply much favoured by government departments and town councils after some desecration of a citizen's rights. Speaking personally, I feel it should be made a criminal offence to reply like that, but I did not invent the system – I am merely pointing out its customs and deficiencies.

Dealing with large firms is more difficult, as their staff have time to cope. So experienced operators write saying that as the matter is complicated it is best discussed *over the phone*. Then they don't even try. People in large organizations don't expect phone calls to get through. Life would be impossible if they did.

With letters like these passing to and fro, correspondence between two Coarse Offices is obviously likely to go round in circles for ever, and plenty of people make a living like that. However, if it is urgently desired to break the circle, go straight to a person at the top. Contact them by name. It sometimes works, and if it doesn't you're no worse off than the rest of suffering humanity.

Plenty of people make a living like that

Internal Communications

The most important form of internal non-communication is the memo. It can be stated without fear of contradiction that the more memos issued, the less the information passed on. One reason is that, when management can think of nothing else to do, they issue a memo. As they can think of nothing else to do most of the time memos have become debased coinage, dealing with trivia at great length.

A favourite one is to announce to the whole world what everybody knows, such as:

International Desecration PLC

Internal Memorandum

From: Head of Personnel Dept. ....

To: All Depts. ....

Subject: Christmas ....

     Christmas Day this year will be on December 25th. Boxing Day will be on December 26th. New Year's Day will be on January 1st. All departments are asked to make arrangements accordingly.

N.B. This does not apply to the Tel Aviv office.

Other memos will contain equally useless information, such as this gem seen recently:

'In the canteen menu, for "carrots" read "tomatoes".'

Some have a habit of treating readers as if they were mentally deficient:

International Desecration PLC

Internal Memorandum

From: ....General Manager.......

To: ....All Depts........

Subject: ....Washroom Designation.......

A new system of designation has been devised in connection with the office washrooms. In the past these have been distinguished by a small silhouette of a member of the appropriate sex, a figure wearing a skirt for the women's facilities and one wearing trousers for those of the men. However, this led to some confusion and embarrassment on the recent visit of the Scottish sales representatives who were wearing kilts. It has therefore been decided to designate the washrooms by a new method. In future, men's washrooms will have on the door a painted sign saying MEN. The women's washrooms will have a similar sign saying WOMEN.

All personnel are asked to familiarise themselves with the new nomenclature and to endeavour to make sure they are using the correct facility. In case of difficulty I can always be contacted on Extension 589.

Memos have now become so prolific we have reached the era of the self-justifying memo – that is, a series devoted entirely to the subject of memos until the noticeboard is filled. Such a board would probably start off with an immensely long memo about the need for brevity. There would be a further one next day:

International Desecration PLC

Internal Memorandum

From: General Manager
....

To: All Depts.
....

Subject: Internal Memoranda
....

   With reference to my memo of yesterday about the vital necessity for memos to be kept to six lines, it has since been pointed out to me that my memo was itself 38 lines long. I should like to observe (a) there are exceptions to the best rules and (b) if anyone wishes to raise a matter of this nature it should be done through the proper channels. The proper channels do not include scrawling 'Your own memo was 38 lines long you loquacious old fart' all over the notice board. Meanwhile, I hope this will not deter authorised persons from using the notice board. I am worried about office communications. Vital decisions are not being passed on.

This will be followed by:

```
Internal Memorandum


From:       General Manager
        ........................

To:         All Depts.
        ........................
Subject:    Internal Memoranda
        ........................
```

       With reference to yesterday's memo about the importance of memos, please ignore, owing to overload on the copying machines. Memoranda must be kept to the minimum.

The above examples contain the classic features of office-board memoranda, namely that they are always contradictory and always out of date. Usually both characteristics appear at the same time. Notices relating to summer holidays, for instance, either appear so early that they are forgotten or else are posted up in September. As last year's memos are still there it's difficult to know what to do. Indeed, I was once with a company where a memo about closing the doors to conserve heat was posted up the day before they were due to demolish the building. It was still there, fluttering in the wind, even when workmen were knocking great holes in the walls.

Thus Law Fifteen of Coarse Business states: If it's on the noticeboard, it can't be important.

The method by which information is transmitted is usually more important than the contents. No matter how important, a letter is liable to be ignored, whereas a telex commands attention. My friend Hicks assures me that when he got tired of nobody attending the annual party he organized at head office, he sent out the invitations by telex. Everybody came. 'We got your telex,' they said, 'and thought we ought to attend.'

If it is absolutely vital something is not communicated, transmit it by electronic methods. Modern computers will easily swallow a fourteen-page report, lose it in the system and spew it out three months later. When technology is ready to help, why resort to lying?

The most commonly used and important form of internal office communication, however, is the old-fashioned message, normally left on the desk of the recipient. This should never be written on an official form or it will be ignored, thrown away or used to wipe up spilt coffee. To catch the eye it may be necessary to adopt weird measures such as writing it on coloured paper in huge characters or pasting it to the recipient's teacup. People go to astonishing lengths to avoid receiving messages. I have actually seen a senior executive sit down on top of an important message which had been placed on the seat of his swivel chair in a last attempt to attract notice.

A secretary I knew used to lay a sort of treasure hunt trail to attract her boss's attention. When he came through the front door of the office the receptionist would say, 'There's a message on your desk, Mr Crawford.' On the mirror in the lift would be scrawled in lipstick: MESSAGE ON YOUR DESK – JENNY. On the door of his room would be a huge poster (MESSAGE ON YOUR DESK) and on the desk a fluorescent arrow pointing to the note. But he became so used to it all that he paid no attention and automatically pushed the message to one side. The only time he noticed was when the trail wasn't there. If that happened he used to seek out his secretary and ask if anybody had left a message.

Much may be deduced from the physical appearance of a message. If there are tea or coffee stains on it, it is important. The sender has interrupted his break to write it down. If immaculately neat, it is unlikely to be important. If the handwriting is shaky and panicky (or the typing full of errors) it will have been written by middle management and will be urgent since they do not soil their fingers with physical labour except under pressure.

The phrasing of a note can provide many clues. It was only after studying messages left by my female boss that I understood she wanted to have an affair with me. Normally she would write cheery little notes such as, 'By the way, Roger rang and said the correct figure is eight million not nine million. Love, Wendy.' I put this informal tone down to friendliness until I realized that whenever a woman rang me her whole attitude changed and she'd scribble, 'Some filthy, sneering bitch with a snooty voice called Beryl rang and said don't forget about tonight. I told her you would be working. Kindly don't take personal calls in the office. Wendy.' In my innocence I didn't appreciate what was going on until she invited me round for dinner. It was a lovely affair. What a pity she married somebody else.

Most people are not very good at expressing themselves clearly, and in an effort at brevity reduce a note to gibberish. When brevity is combined with jargon the results are incomprehensible, such as the note my friend Askew claims to have received from a senior man: 'Interface 3 o'clock. J.B.'

Askew replied in similar vein with a message: 'Uninterface 3 o'clock. Dentist. Reinterface 4 p.m. J.A.'

This was a wise wheeze of Askew's, since one receives little credit in an office for plain English. How you say something is so much more important than what is said, and even a scribbled message couched in rubbish terms may win the sender a Brownie point. Plain language or simple English tends to make executives wince.

To survive, it is necessary to be able to translate the special speech which is used. This bears as much relation to normal talk as Sanskrit does to English, because office language is used as a means not of communication but of defence. Thus the meaning will probably be the opposite of what is actually said. Here are some phrases commonly used to callers in person or on the phone, together with a translation:

He's just popped out	He's in Florida
He's in conference He's got someone with him	He doesn't want to talk
He's busy at the moment	He's having coffee
He's out of the building	He's in the building
Can I get him to call you back?	Then he can forget about it
Can his secretary help?	You're not important enough to speak direct
I'll just see if he's free	You may be slightly more important than I thought you were – I'll check
Would you like to speak to someone else instead?	No, you weren't important
Who did you say you were?	Another whiner
Michael who?	You're nobody

I remember calling at a West End office recently where I could see the person I wanted to speak to through a ground-floor window. He was sitting at his desk doing nothing, so I bounded in and asked to see him.

'He's away all this week,' said the receptionist, giving me that special stare they have for people they don't like.

'Look, he can't be,' I protested. 'I have just looked through his window and seen him.'

'He's away all week,' she repeated.

'Are you sure? Perhaps he's sneaked back unexpectedly.'

31

'I'll just try, but I know he's away.' She fiddled with her switchboard. 'Yes, there's no reply. He's away.'

I went outside. My friend was still there at his desk, so I shouted through the open window.

He looked up. 'Mike! What are you doing here? Why don't you go round the front and come in?'

I explained I'd already tried that without success. To avoid further embarrassment I climbed in through the window, although the receptionist was rather surprised when we left together for lunch.

Most of the phrases quoted so far are defence against outsiders, but there is another branch of office non-communication used as an internal weapon against colleagues. Here are some useful phrases, with translation, which can be employed in either speech or writing:

I think we should	I think *you* should
It appears to me	Somebody else says
There is a strong body of opinion	I think
Some opposition to	I don't like it
It could be argued that	But I hope no one will be foolish enough to do so
While not wishing to	I wish to vehemently
Sound out opinion	I can't make up my mind
We should beware of the consequences	Don't blame me, old man
It has been pointed out	Some dirty bastard has put in the knife

The House Magazine and Employee Relations

The house magazine or company newspaper has a big role in non-communication. Its purpose is not to inform employees about what is going on but to inform them about what is *not* going on. The real news in any organization, the seething discontent at the works, the back-stabbing on the board, the terrible fraud at head office, the scandal in the accounts department, will all be ignored. Instead the readers will be treated to a long account of how head office dramatic society are producing *Oklahoma*, and they hope this year the curtain won't fall in the middle of the second act as it did last time. The only news from the simmering hotbed of revolution at the factory is that Sam Perkins, of sheet metal, has got a pigeon which goes faster than all the other pigeons. The fact that one bird was found nailed to his front door with the word 'Scab' painted on its wings is carefully omitted.

The same approach is visible in other forms of employee information. It is summed up by a man I worked for who said quite sincerely, 'I believe in communication as long as I don't have to talk to people.' He meant it, too. This firm had a video tape explaining the annual accounts which it showed in a continuous loop on a TV set in the canteen. For twenty-four hours a day, seven days a week it broadcast its message for three months, to an unheeding audience queuing up for fish and chips. Admittedly, this company had a bad history of non-communication. It was said that even the rumours travelled slowly.

I mention this because a COP must never make the mistake of suggesting to senior staff that they actually talk to their employees. Communication between management and staff must be by remote means such as magazines, videos and posters. Ideally, a firm will pay a public relations consultancy a high fee for organizing this non-communication.

Try to keep out of the house magazine. It's the kiss of death to appear in it. Colleagues regard you as a sycophantic creep or are jealous; management are suspicious that you may be a publicity-seeker. I once had a colleague who saved two little children from drowning on holiday, although there wasn't much danger as the water was only four feet deep. Foolishly, he allowed the house magazine to report the fact under the headline:

'COMPANY MAN HERO OF SEASIDE DRAMA'.

His life was not worth living after that. He would be greeted in the office with alleged funny remarks such as 'Hello, hero, saved anyone from drowning today?' Management became very suspicious, and his departmental head was heard to say that if *he* saved anyone from drowning in four feet of water he'd keep it quiet – he wouldn't go rushing round plastering it all over the company paper. So much for heroism.

If it is really necessary to spread information swiftly and efficiently, the best method of doing so is to start a rumour. The most effective manner of doing this is to tell the commissionaire, the receptionist or the switchboard and swear them to secrecy.

3

Getting a Job

I like work; it fascinates me. I can sit and look at it for hours. I love to keep it by me: the idea of getting rid of it nearly breaks my heart.
Jerome K. Jerome

In British industry, the finest qualification for a senior post is to have failed in a similar job elsewhere. What happens to a chairman or managing director whose incompetence has ruined a company? Is he sent packing without a penny and refused further employment? No, he's paid off with a huge sum and immediately gets a highly rewarded post on someone else's board. When firms are willing to pay well for men who have failed spectacularly it is no wonder the country's economy is up the creek. It's a miracle it ever had the strength even to get up the creek.

Unfortunately, it's only at senior level that having been sacked is a recommendation. And to have been made redundant, rather than being sacked, in the junior ranks is even worse. It suggests that the applicant wasn't worth firing but is just another piece of commercial cannon fodder. So the first task of someone seeking employment in a Coarse Office – unless it is their first job – is to have ready an explanation as to why they left the previous firm. So many are made redundant these days that the question may not even be raised. But if it is, remember that whining about what a disaster redundancy was – 'I've got to have a job or I'll starve' – will get you nowhere. 'Laugh and the world laughs with you; weep and you weep alone,' said Ella Wheeler Wilcox in the last century, and she had obviously just been made redundant.

Don't say something negative such as, 'The departmental head didn't like me.' Blame your previous employers. 'They lost three million last year. They were getting rid of staff right and left.' If necessary be self-righteous. 'They asked me to pass a dishonest expenses sheet. You have to draw the line somewhere.' (This last statement might not be a recommendation in some places.)

A factor which inhibits many people seeking work is the fear that some career detail will spoil their chances: 'I hope they won't find out I was expelled from technical college', or 'I'm terrified they'll discover the truth about my shorthand.' These fears are usually exaggerated. Applications aren't studied that closely. I once wrote for a post and worried myself sick because I found I'd spelled the firm's name wrongly. Not only was I asked for an interview but their reply repeated my incorrect spelling. Another time I answered the wrong box number and still got called for interview for a job that was nothing like the one I'd applied for. I think I might even have got it, if I had persevered.

A great deal depends on how matters are phrased in the CV. There is no career disaster that cannot be turned to advantage by a skilled hand and here is a simple example which will explain all:

Coarse Office Person's CV

CV	TRUTH
While working for Blenkinsop's I was twice made Salesman of the Year	I was the only salesman they'd got
I suggested a reorganization of the staff which saved £12,000 a year	I shopped a colleague over his expenses and they fired him

CV	**TRUTH**
I was in charge of all retail sales	I was the only assistant in the shop
At college I was very active in the amateur dramatic society	I slept with the stage manager
I passed my degree finals at university in medieval English	I failed the other seven papers
I was treasurer of the office social committee	I organized the tea money

A few such well-chosen phrases and your application will stand out from the common herd, who are writing negative stuff such as, 'Although I was thrown out of comprehensive school for arson and sexual offences, my headmaster said I was very good at geography.' Note that there are no direct lies in the chart. Lying is a filthy and illegal practice. Why lie when a little bullshit will get even further?

But remember: If a box number is quoted, check it is not your own job which you apply for. My friend Askew claims he once did this after seeing it advertised. It was described as: 'A challenging, well-paid post, for a man who is not afraid to make decisions and who wants a chance to rise to the top.' It sounded so attractive he applied at once. Furthermore he almost got the job. He received a very enthusiastic letter calling him for interview, only by then he had realized what had occurred and withdrew. Then came the problem: 'Why are they advertising my job?' The answer came in a few weeks when his boss told him, 'To be frank, old chap, we advertised your job *but we couldn't get anyone satisfactory.* The only man fit for the job withdrew at the last minute. Funny thing – he had a name like yours.'

With luck the applicant will be called for interview. (It is possible to tell from the reply envelope whether it is good or bad news – the rejects come by second-class post.) If possible, try to

37

find out what the interview room looks like, perhaps with a quick glance through the door when someone comes out, or by asking the receptionist. The layout must affect an applicant's approach. Some years ago I decided to give up work and apply for a job lecturing at a university. I thought the positive approach would be best, and when called before the board I flung open the door booming, 'Good morning, gentlemen'. Unfortunately the room was so tiny that the panel were seated three feet in front of me and I nearly burst their eardrums, apart from crashing the door violently against a filing cabinet. My outstretched hand hit the chairman in the face. There appeared on their faces the sort of polite but pained expression that academics specialize in, a sort of 'Oh-dear-there's-a-bad-smell' look, and I knew I was doomed before I had even begun. As a last desperate effort to impress them I tried to say goodbye in Latin, muttering 'Bonus Matinus, gentlemen, as they said in Rome', but they were not impressed.

A big interview room can be an even greater hazard. The candidate opens a door timidly to find there is about a hundred yards to progress before reaching the panel. This completely spoils any attempt at making an effective entrance. It's not much use bounding into the room shouting, 'Good morning, all,' when the board can hardly hear you, let alone see your face.

If it is exceptionally large be sure to take note of the way back. The Civil Service in particular are fond of holding interviews in vast areas intended for seating five hundred persons. Poor Askew had a terrible experience during one of his many unavailing efforts to enter the Civil Service (my opinion of the Civil Service rose when they wouldn't employ Askew). He was being interviewed in what he insisted was the Banqueting Hall of Whitehall Palace, but which may have been somewhere slightly smaller. The panel were seated with their backs to a huge window through which the sun was streaming and Askew was forced to grope blindly forward for about fifty yards before establishing contact. After half an hour's close cross-examination he was utterly exhausted and confused (lying imposes a great mental strain), and when the time came to leave he discovered he'd forgotten the way out. There were three doors and he couldn't possibly remember the one by which he'd entered. Not wishing to give the board the impression he was indecisive as well as stupid and dishonest, he chose one of them and strode firmly up to it. On reaching the door he turned and said, 'I bid you all good day, gentlemen', grasped the handle, opened the door, and marched through it.

Unfortunately, it was the broom cupboard.

With masterly presence of mind Askew kept his head, pulled the door behind him and remained there while the other candidates were interviewed.

Conduct during the interview itself is most important. One of the biggest problems is when a candidate has invented a fictitious career and forgets what it was.

'Tell us more about Foundry Pressings,' says one of the interviewers. 'What was your exact position?'

A terrible blank comes over the applicant. Who are Foundry Pressings? Did I really say that? Oh yes, he means Basingstoke. What on earth did I claim to have done? Was I in charge of production or overseas sales? The result is that the applicant frequently asks the questions, probing with queries like, 'I think I was in charge of customer relations, wasn't I?' On seeing the blank looks all round he hastily changes the reply to 'No, no, I don't mean customer relations – I mean UK marketing, I think . . . I hope . . . what does it say there?' Desperate at this point, he gets up and peers over the interviewer's shoulder.

Unless the applicant is one of those happy people blessed with total recall and self-confidence, there is only one way out of the difficulty and that is to have a copy of your CV in front of you. If this should invite remarks such as, 'Can't you remember your own career?' reply firmly, 'The man who relies on memory for important facts is the man who makes mistakes, as they say at the Harvard Business School.'

Remember that those conducting interviews are at an even greater loss than the person seeking the job. That is why they ask stupid questions such as, 'If you get this post, what improvements will you make?' Avoid the temptation to answer rubbish questions with rubbish answers like 'If you don't know what's wrong with the organization after running it for twenty years, you can't expect me to tell you in five minutes.'

Other lunatic questions will probably include:

Why do you want this job? (Don't reply: Because it's nearer the underground station or the work looks easy. Say: Because you need a challenge.)

Why do you want to leave your present job? (Don't say: Because you had a row with the boss. Say: The firm is out of date.)

What will you expect from your colleagues? (Don't say: You expect everyone to love you and buy you drinks. Say: I expect nothing. It's what *they* expect from *me* that matters.)

Don't worry about not appearing to best advantage. Interviewers aren't nearly as observant as you think. A girlfriend went for an interview for a teaching post and her knickers dropped off just as she sat down. She was sitting close to the table and by judicious wriggling got them over her shoes and kicked them under the table where they lay sneering at her throughout the interview. Nobody noticed, although the cleaner probably wondered what had been going on. She got the job. 'Actually,' she said later, 'I think most of the panel were so old they didn't recognize them.'

In fact they aren't usually interested in the answer. Even if an applicant did say what was wrong with the organization in ten seconds they wouldn't believe it. They just feel they have to say something. The way the reply is given is more important than the reply itself, so speak drivel as if you meant it. Once I had to sit on a panel interviewing people for a job. The first candidate

Those conducting interviews are at an even greater loss than the person
seeking the job

was a girl with thick pebble glasses and a first-class honours degree in linguistics. She smoked continuously, swore, scratched herself, broke wind loudly and dropped ash on the carpet, but was obviously the most intelligent person in the room. They gave the job to a man with one of those phoney fixed grins and firm handshakes you learn in the School of Salesmanship and he lasted six months.

Never admit to having worked with your hands. Class traditions die hard, which is why a bad army officer is given an admin. post in civil life and a good sergeant is offered the commissionaire's job. To say you had a year on the shop floor of an engineering works can just about finish any hope of a white-collar position.

If nepotism is involved, don't give way to over-confidence. Do not rush in shouting, 'Hello, uncle, good to see you. When can I start?' Others may be jealous and wish to have their own relative appointed. Askew is still haunted by a terrible experience when he thought he had a job fixed up with a friend. Between them they had even decided what sort of a car he would have. He leaped into the room for interview, winked at his pal and said, 'Right then, where are you going to put my desk?' His friend was not as influential as he thought, and Askew was rejected. 'And after all the beer I bought him at the golf club,' moaned Askew. 'It makes you lose faith in human nature.'

Strangely enough, the public sector is a stronghold of nepotism. Many posts advertised so freely have already been privately filled. When I worked in the Civil Service I went for a promotion board and met another candidate in the waiting room. 'I'm sorry to tell you, old man,' he said, 'that you are not going to get this job. I've been told it's mine, as I've been here longer. But I'm assured you'll get the next one.' So six people were solemnly interviewed and sure enough he was appointed. However, since the public sector, however corrupt, has to keep up appearances, make no reference to the fact that it's all fixed.

Otherwise they may feel a fit of morality and appoint another.

At some point the applicant will be asked if there's anything they'd like to know. Be careful. If a decision is teetering in the balance it could be the last straw to ask, 'Is it possible to leave at 4.30 every evening so I can catch the train? And how long do we get at Christmas? And can you get early retirement at fifty?'

When the time comes to leave, men should be prepared for a masonic handshake. If not a mason do not attempt to reply by imitating it. Do not say, 'I didn't know you were a judo expert.' Do not think it is a homosexual advance and encourage him by winking and grimacing. Presumably masons will know what to do. Others ignore it. And if the man's hands are sweaty don't wipe yours on your coat. Note: If a woman receives what feels like a masonic handshake she should ask herself what is wrong with her appearance.

An important problem in seeking a job is that advertisements are written in adspeak jargon by people who are illiterate, so it is not easy to know what they mean. For example: 'The position will suit someone who has a proven record in motivating and managing the human resource and who is able to optimize the initiation of special projects which are end-user orientated.' (This means they want an area sales manager.) Fortunately, the advertisement is usually headlined with the real title of the post and this will give a clue as to what it is all about. Reply in similar gibberish ('I have consistently implemented the role of maximizing work-orientation. . . .') But don't be carried away and overdo it. My poor Uncle Walter, in an effort to be up-to-date, once wrote a pathetic letter for a rep's job saying, 'I am married with two human resources at a local school . . .' and was not called for interview. 'I thought they would have liked that touch, my boy,' he used to say, wistfully.

Be careful not to be deceived by adspeak into thinking the job is more important than it really is. Remember that 'motivating the human resource' may well mean stopping people smoking in the washrooms.

It may sound unlikely advice in these days of high unemployment, but be careful of any job where the potential employer tries to sell the post. Some jobs are worse than none at all. I once went for a selling job in Birmingham. It was not advertised as such – in fact the advertisement referred to 'an opportunity for a well-educated and motivated man to earn a fortune in the academic field' – so I went along and was greeted by a man with a moustache that oozed distrust and a piercing eye straight from the Manual of Selling. He talked for ten minutes non-stop about the job, which was selling encyclopedias, one of those awful commission-only jobs where you make a fortune the first month out of your friends and go broke afterwards when they are all stuffed to the attics with books. But he wouldn't tell me there was no salary.

'Salary?' he boomed when I asked him. 'I prefer to use the term "reward". The rewards are endless, boundless, limitless. Remember, this encyclopedia is the product of twenty-six universities. There is no limit to what you can earn.'

'But how much do I get every month?'

'How much would you like? Name any figure and it's yours.'

I tried to turn down the job but he wouldn't let me. 'Michael,' he kept saying, 'I do not believe you are going to reject the opportunity to be rich.'

'Yes I am,' I said hastily as I reached the door. 'Don't ring me, I'll ring you.'

Another bait offered by dubious employers is sex, for both men and women. I have seen girl secretaries offered the lure of marriage by a businessman who used to say, 'You'll be the only girl in the room as the rest are men, but you won't mind that, eh? Our last three girls all left to get married, so you might be lucky. . . .' All this accompanied by a hideous nudge, nudge, wink, wink.

Men are sometimes offered the prospect of an endless sexual orgy if they will only sign up. 'As you can see, we have lots of pretty girls here and most of them seem pretty willing, don't they, Janice? If you don't pick up something at the Christmas party it'll be your own fault. . . .'

This sort of employer is usually rather vague about the pension scheme. However, it is some consolation to know you can have unceasing sexual intercourse until the age of sixty-five, even if you won't have anything to live on afterwards.

The worst interview is the selection process that goes on for three days, or even three weeks, in which candidates are incarcerated in a country house and their every move watched, from the way they drink their coffee to whether they pick their nose. Large organizations are especially prone to this. A friend in a bank who was sent to one of these places to see if he was top-management material was so scared (rumours said they spied on candidates to see if they had unpleasant nocturnal habits) that he was petrified with fear. He was worried about his table manners, since he was a jovial eater who sprayed gravy all over the table and ate peas with his spoon, and he knew people were closely watched at meals. He decided to avoid eating completely. It was a forty-eight-hour grilling and by Sunday night he was ravenous, having lived only on chocolate, but with a spotless reputation. Unfortunately they held a cocktail party to mark the end of the course, and having a completely empty stomach he collapsed, babbling, after three gins and had to be helped from the room under the eyes of the principal and staff. He failed.

Never confide in anyone, not even a fellow interviewee. They may be spies. My friend who got drunk revealed how one candidate told a female cleaner what a stupid idea the whole thing was and how he'd cheated in some test, and it turned out she was a senior member of staff. Apparently she posed as an old dear and made friends with candidates and encouraged them to tell her their troubles and then wrote a secret report.

If any of the above seems cynical or exaggerated, permit me to quote from the *Financial Times* of 6 September 1984, commenting on a survey of recruitment in British industry conducted by

. . . had to be helped babbling from the room

Brunel University: 'For while the employers' approaches to recruiting were bewilderingly varied, the survey suggests that snobbery, along with cowardice and a kind of nepotism, remain alive and kicking in the top offices of British industry, commerce, professions and public services.'

Who am I to quarrel with that?

4

Office Relationships and Power Structure

Unlimited power is apt to corrupt the minds of those who possess it.
William Pitt

Rank in an office is taken from the person an employee works for, rather than from their own status, like the Victorian servants' halls where a duke's valet outranked a knight's maid and all sat at table in strict order of seniority. So the marketing director's deputy may well be less important than the chairman's secretary. Because people are identified with their boss two departments sometimes won't talk to each other if their chiefs have quarrelled. It is said that a famous firm of publishers went under after a row between the head of publicity and the editorial director, so the advertising campaign bore no relation to the books they intended bringing out, since none of the staff would communicate. They even sat at different ends of the canteen. The ultimate in this must surely be the experience of an English firm with two German subsidiary companies, which feuded so badly they actually sued each other and head office had to step in.

But rank also depends on the view of the beholder. The organization chart which a company produces has nothing at all to do with the real power structure. It is the first precaution of a COP to identify the real power points in an office. These are probably not the departmental heads or directors but such widely scattered people as the telex operator, the receptionist,

1. Conventional Power Structure

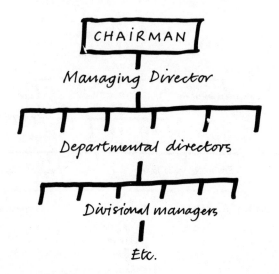

the switchboard girl, the tea trolley lady and the man who fixes broken typewriters and replaces the electric light bulbs.

The diagrams illustrate the point. The first shows a conventional business power structure with authority flowing downwards from the chairman to the minions below; the second shows the same system as viewed by the cleaner; the third is the power structure from a secretary's viewpoint; and the fourth shows the organization as viewed by the chairman himself.

The interesting thing about the cleaner's view of rank is that the whole set-up has become inverted. The lower down the office scale one is, the less important do people at the top become. To those immediately around him, such as his assistants, the chairman is a figure of awe, the man with 10,000 jobs in his hands and millions of pounds to spend. To the cleaners he's just a miserable old sod who knocks out his pipe in the wastepaper basket and who has a nasty habit of throwing used tissues on the floor. I shall never forget emerging shaken

2. Cleaner's Power Structure

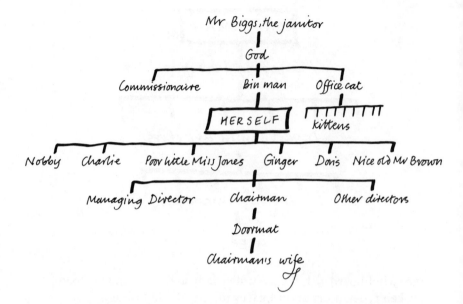

from the office of an editor of one of the world's greatest newspapers (well, how was I to know Ankara wasn't the capital of Jordan?). As I stood outside, mopping my brow and making V-signs at the door, a twenty-year-old lout of a courier, complete with crash helmet and leathers, barged in shouting, 'Come on guv, where's that bleedin' document you was in such a hurry to have sent off?'

To lower ranks, the important persons are their immediate superiors. To a sales rep, the marketing director is king; the tea-trolley lady thinks nothing of abusing him for not returning his cup. A cleaner thinks the caretaker is the most powerful person in the office, slightly above the Almighty. He allocates the soap and buckets, he dishes out the jobs, he hires and fires her. Then come the commissionaire, and someone rather unlikely, such as The Man Who Empties the Big Bin (this is because she can't do

3. Secretary's Power Structure

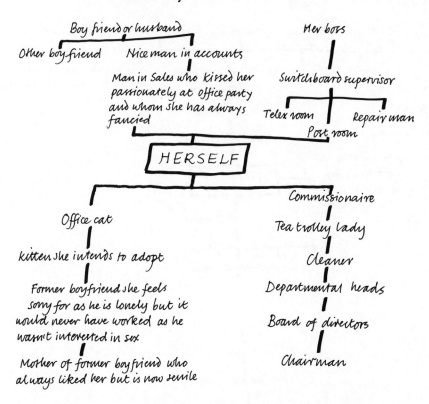

Boy friend or husband

Other boyfriend   Nice man in accounts

Man in Sales who kissed her
passionately at office party
and whom she has always
fancied

Her boss

Switchboard supervisor

Telex room   Repair man

Post room

HERSELF

Commissionaire

Office cat

Tea trolley lady

kitten she intends to adopt

Cleaner

Former boyfriend she feels
sorry for as he is lonely but it
would never have worked as he
wasn't interested in sex

Departmental heads

Board of directors

Mother of former boyfriend who
always liked her but is now senile

Chairman

it herself when he turns nasty and won't). On the same level is
the office cat. Below her, the cleaner has a line of people she
quite likes, frequently because she feels sorry for them, like nice
old Mr Rowlands everyone has a down on. The usual run of
higher management are not important. She can offend the
chairman with impunity, bursting into his room when he's
working late and calling out, 'Look at that pipe ash all over the
bleedin' carpet. Ain't you got no manners in 'ere?' The mighty
chairman's wife figures only as someone who once walked over
a bit of floor she'd just washed and didn't say sorry.

51

4. Chairman's Power Structure

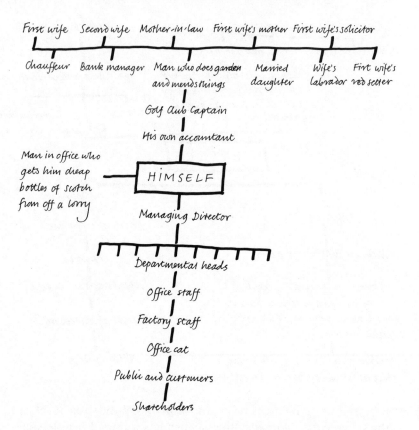

The secretary's power scheme is chaotic, because she has two loyalties, one to her boss and the other to her private life, and there is a constant battle between the two. When I worked for a car company I shared an office with an awfully nice girl in her thirties who had managed to get her life into the sort of tangle secretaries seem to specialize in. The whole set-up was summarized by her shopping bag: it was a basket piled full of tragedy. On top would be some special dainty food for her old,

The usual run of higher management are not important

dying dog, which should have been put down as he had kidney failure, but she couldn't bring herself to do it. There would also be something tasty for her husband's evening meal. He was a miserable old stick but she was fond of him and looked after him tenderly since his heart attack. She was also carrying on a sort of affair with a younger man but I don't think it got very far because his health was even worse than her husband's, so underneath her husband's chicken breasts might be some kidneys for him. His old mother lived alone, gibbering and salivating inside her walking frame, so the secretary also bought a bottle of sherry for her. The poor girl was worn out with emotional entanglements and at the same time was devoted to her boss because he had an unhappy home life and she felt sorry for him, too. She didn't buy him things, she just stayed late.

Not all secretaries are so complicated, of course. But whatever the outside distractions are, whether it's the operatic society, the boyfriends or her cat (usually the cat), there is a whole network of priorities running parallel with those of the office.

Those sections of the office power structure which affect daily life are the secretary's priority, chiefly the switchboard, the telex room, the post room and the maintenance man. Someone who can mend her desk lamp or fix the typewriter is obviously more important than the chairman or managing director, whom most staff never see unless they have the horror of sharing a lift with them. (Law 46 of Coarse Office Life: There is no more embarrassing experience on earth than being trapped in a lift with a senior executive. All conversation ceases and a ghastly silence ensues. Often everybody tries to get out at the first opportunity, whether it's their floor or not.)

Just occasionally there crops up a secretary with only one priority – her boss. These dedicated women admit to only one lord and ruler in the office and regard everybody else as an unwelcome intrusion. A few years ago I was walking through a firm's office with the chairman when a girl passed us. She went pale at the sight of the chairman, stuck her nose in the air and flounced by without a word. 'That's the personnel manager's secretary,' said the chairman. 'She won't speak to me ever since I told off her boss.' There is no point in drawing a chart for these single-minded girls as it would have only one name on it.

I have, of course, assumed secretaries to be female. The male secretary is still a rarity.

Even the chairman's view of the power structure is different from the official sequence. In theory there is no one above him; in practice there are two formidable figures, his wife and mother-in-law, whose baleful influence is linked with the dominance of the chauffeur and the bank manager, while in the background there will be hangovers from a previous marriage or two. Don't underestimate the chauffeur's power. I once worked for a company whose chairman spent his life flying on awkward air routes because his chauffeur wouldn't drive to Heathrow: he didn't like the traffic. He tried to force the chauffeur to drive to Heathrow, but he drove so slowly they missed the plane. The result was the unhappy executive had to fly from Gatwick, Stansted or Luton. The service from Luton to Japan is not very good, and frequently he had to switch planes at Amsterdam.

The chairman's wife is a key figure in most companies. She is the office bane. Her influence is enormous and disastrous. There is a factory in West London which was painted a ghastly shade of pink because the chairman's wife thought it would look nice. People wince as they pass; motorists stare and crash their cars. Furthermore, the lady insisted on the installation of a vast tank of fish in the entrance hall ('You need something warm and vital in Reception, Robert . . .'). Unfortunately, disease struck the fish and visitors were treated to the warm and vital sight of dead fish floating belly-upwards all over one wall.

Invariably, the chairman's lady thinks she knows more about matters of design and taste than do the professionals.

Teams of skilled people toil over a product and produce three possible versions. The chairman shows the drawings to his wife at the weekend down in Hampshire. 'I don't like any of them,' she says, 'you want something more . . . more . . . more . . . .' She can rarely express herself concisely but perhaps sketches what she means. Invariably this is exactly the same as the competitor's latest model. If it is a chocolate box it will look like Black Magic. All chocolate boxes designed by chairman's wives look like Black Magic (Law Three of Coarse Office Life). The chairman returns to the office and tells the designers, 'I've been talking to my wife about this. She knows about these things. I mean she did a course at Ealing Tech. once. She's got an instinctive flair. She feels none of these are quite . . . quite . . . well, anyway, here's what she thinks it should look like.'

He produces the sketch which looks exactly like the competition. At this point the wise COP designer does not draw attention to the fact but says: How very interesting, she must be extremely talented, you are a lucky man, sir, and goes away to tear up her sketches.

Chairmen's wives are particularly prone to interfere in the design of logos and emblems. They feel they have a talent for these things. That is why thousands of firms have the same sort of ill-designed chairman's wife logo, something that always contains wings and probably wheels and an arrow as well. This will be plastered over everything from lorries to letterhead.

Coming to the bottom of the chairman's chart, it will be noticed that the very dregs are the company shareholders, a little lower than the general public. It is arguable which come lower, but the shareholders just win. Only a shareholder can fully appreciate this. Having scraped together a few pounds against old age he invests it in a company, to see the chairman reduce it to bankruptcy and leave with a huge golden handshake as his reward, paid at the expense of shareholders and employees. While industry rewards failure so lavishly, why should anyone try to be successful?

Perhaps the most important power source in any office is the chief executive's secretary. These ladies have usually had a brain transplant as a result of which they see life in terms of their employer. If told an atomic bomb has just exploded they will reply, 'Oh dear, that means Mr Grimshaw won't be able to keep his lunch appointment.' Never be flippant at their hero's expense. Remarks like 'I see the old idiot's taking yet another day off again' will be taken as a personal insult. Play it their way. Sympathize with the employer's difficulties. 'No wonder he's away, with all the problems he's had recently. Tell me, is his smoked salmon poisoning any better?' Yet top secretaries may have a kind heart beneath the frigid exterior. They are frequently susceptible to motherly feelings. Say you feel terrible, that's the worst of living alone, there's nobody to look after you, look at my coat all covered in dandruff, I only had a tin of baked beans for dinner last night. This may soften them up. Never quarrel with them. They guard the portals of power and nobody passes in without their permission. If you wish to be a failure in life, offend the chief executive's secretary.

Coarse Titles

How a person is addressed in the office gives a clue to status. As they might say in a business studies exam, comment on the difference between the following modes of address:

1. Mike has just returned from a successful sales trip.
2. I'm afraid Michael has a drink problem.
3. We are sacking Miss Wilkins.
4. You'll just love J.B.
5. Tell Bloggins to clean up the mess.
6. Ask Ginger to bring round the car.
7. We are transferring the girl with big boobs.
8. Fatarse is on the prowl again.

Note the difference between a contracted first name and the more formal version. Mike, Gerry or Liz are signs of good status and confidence but the usage changes to Michael, Gerald and Elizabeth when trouble looms. To be referred to by initials only is the highest mode of address, the commercial equivalent of calling a peer by his title – Winchester, Salisbury or Leicester say.

A surname for the unhappy Miss Wilkins and the downtrodden Bloggins is self-explanatory. Not long ago all girls were Miss (or Mrs) and all men called by surnames. It was no disgrace then, but all has now changed and if people insist on addressing you by the surname something is wrong, except in the remoter reaches of the Foreign Office. These days the use of a surname causes intense irritation and it is a good wheeze for the COP who wishes to upset somebody. A friend in the car industry used to infuriate his enemies by calling them Green, Smith and Jones.

The use of a nickname such as Ginger shows low status but good position. Nobody senior is ever called Ginger or Nobby. On the other hand, a person called by a nickname has established a safe niche. Nobby is rarely sacked; Mr Clark may well be.

It is doom to be referred to by a physical attribute. I have quoted The Girl with the Big Boobs, but it could equally well be The Chap with the Bald Head or The Man with the Big Stomach. Once you're The Person with the Funny Something you are finished, my friend. It is never flattering attributes that are picked on. Even Big Boobs is used derogatively, and nobody ever gets called The Man with the Nice Face or The Girl with the Sweet Smile.

The ultimate form of address is to be known by an unpleasant nickname (Stinky, Rotguts, Fatarse, etc.). This is reserved almost entirely for unpopular lower management and is rarely bestowed unless deserved.

In the more formal days of yesteryear it was possible for a

person's title to go through a complete circle in their working life. On starting as office boy, Gerald Smith would be known to his superiors as Gerry; when a bit older it would be Gerald; on promotion to junior clerk it became Smith. When Smith got to managerial level he was called Mr Smith but once on the board his fellow directors called him Gerald. Eventually, as chairman, he reverted to the original title of Gerry, with employees calling him Mr Gerry.

A similar progression was possible for a girl, starting as Betty Smith the typist, and passing through Elizabeth the secretary to Mrs Bradshaw the supervisor and finally back to Betty if she got on the board, although such heights were rare for a woman in those days.

Today, except in some nineteenth-century relic companies, address by the first name is common, with Mr for senior people. Since it is very difficult to alter a name once people get stuck with it, it's best to be firm about your title from the start. Otherwise the COP may be landed with a nickname like Stinky for the next ten years.

Approach to Senior Management

One of the chief tasks in a Coarse Office will be to protect senior management from the realities of life. It is best to consider the boss as incapable of even the simplest action such as pouring his own coffee, writing letters or booking a hotel room (there was an advert in the *Daily Telegraph* this morning saying 'Tell your secretary to cut out this coupon'). Further, like a child, a management executive is liable to wallow in his own filth. I don't mean senior staff need nappies (although some do) but they leave tidying up to others. For years I worked in the next room to a senior man who was always complaining about his coffee cup. When first a little brown ring appeared round the inside he started to whine about the state of the office coffee

59

cups. Note the plural. They manage to translate individual matters to the world at large. If a boss's coffee cup is dirty, everybody's cup is dirty. Gradually the stain got bigger (his regular secretary was away). Eventually the cup was like something off a building site, brown inside, chipped round the rim and with green bubbles in the bottom. Yet not once did it occur to him to clean it out or buy a new one. He just sat there complaining until his secretary returned and bought him a new one and he was all smiles again. Typically, he decided that all the coffee cups were now clean. 'I see the coffee cups are much cleaner these days,' he beamed.

Helplessness is a disease of senior male staff (women executives are more self-reliant). A friend in the Civil Service was telling me the other day that a brigadier seconded to his department fell ill at home but couldn't tell the office as he didn't know the phone number. While it is horrifying to think of the country being run by people who don't even know the phone number of their own office, it's not unusual. The quickest way to the sack is to tell a senior person to do something himself.

Among the menaces senior people must be protected from are the public and customers. Many businesses exist not to serve the public but to serve themselves, and that also applies to large sections of the Civil Service and local government. The public are an unwelcome intrusion. I reached that conclusion years ago when the jack supplied with my new car bent the first time I used it. I posted it back to the makers asking for an explanation, and all they could reply was that it had been tested in the laboratory to umpteen thousand square inches and I must have been operating it wrongly. However the design *had* been changed. I wrote back pointing out that the jack had to be used not in a laboratory but by the side of the M1 in pouring rain; and if it was so satisfactory why had they changed the design? To no avail, I need hardly add.

Industry's ideal situation is to sell their products to the

Helplessness is a disease of senior male staff

people who supply the raw materials, so that nobody else is involved at all. Thus Law 17 of Coarse Office Life says: When dealing with the public never admit to being wrong. It is a hard rule but there is no thanks for breaking it. I shan't forget working for a company where one of the staff actually wrote apologizing to a customer and the MD saw the letter. He burst into the room waving it and shouting, 'Which bloody idiot wrote this?'

A typical letter which will satisfy management might be as follows:

> Dear Madam,
>
> I am sorry to hear you were injured in an explosion when switching on our product. From your description it seems likely you did not follow the correct operating instructions, described in the leaflet enclosed with the apparatus. I enclose a fresh leaflet since you say the original was burned in the fire which destroyed your house.
>
> I hope you recover your sight shortly. Perhaps you could get a friend to read this letter to you.
>
> Assuring you of our best attention at all times.
>
> Yours faithfully,

Of course in nationalized industries, such as British Gas, it is not necessary to reply to a customer's letter at all.

Senior management regard personal contact with a customer as the Ultimate Horror, one degree worse than having to meet someone from the factory floor. Even if it is only a letter of complaint, they hastily pass it down the line. It is pitiful to watch them crying for help when cornered by a customer. My neighbour's wife bought a washing machine one Friday and it broke down next day. This machine was made by a company named after its founder and chairman, so being a determined woman she traced the chairman's home number and rang him.

'Your washing machine has broken down,' she explained.

'How do you mean, mine?'

'Well it's got your name in big letters right across the front of it, so I presume it's yours.'

'But what do you want me to do about it?'

'I want you to give me some advice. I'm in the middle of a week's wash for a family of six. If I tell you what's wrong will you tell me how to put it right? Or would you come over and mend it?'

This last suggestion was followed by a long silence and then the phone was angrily put down. So protect seniors from personal contact with customers at all times. Under no circumstances must management meet the persons they are selling to.

Paradoxically, in a Coarse Office it does no harm to be a friend to someone the department head does not like. Apart from the fact that it's a pleasant gesture in a cruel world, it gets under the boss's skin. They can't understand anybody being pally with a person they don't approve of. It worries them. They feel insecure. 'I can't understand what you see in that fellow Jackson,' they say with a worried frown. One characteristic of management is they want everyone to think like they do, and the exception makes them feel they have failed.

General Hints on Survival for the COP

O let us love our occupations
Bless the squire and his relations,
Live upon our daily rations,
And always know our proper stations.
Dickens

The first essential of Coarse Office survival is always to look busy. This applies at all levels. It's as important for senior staff to appear overwhelmed as it is for clerks or sales reps. In some ways it is more important for senior people, otherwise they lose one of their chief levers against their subordinates, namely that they don't work hard enough. It looks bad for a director to mumble, 'My God, I wish I only worked from nine to five,' as he staggers down the steps of the Café Royal at half-past three.

I learned this Law on a newspaper in Northampton. My best friend was employed at the Kettering office, some miles away, and being remote from head office was left to his own devices. There wasn't much doing in Kettering in those days apart from an occasional case of sexual perversion (usually with sheep) at the local court so he had plenty of time for his hobby, which was making model ships and putting them into bottles. It became an obsession. First he filled the mantelpiece, then he hung them on the walls, and finally they took over his desk. One day the editor decided to pay a visit and marched into the office on a Thursday afternoon. The first thing that happened was he crunched underfoot a two-foot model of a tea clipper; the second was he broke a finger on my friend's hand, because he was on the floor working on it. The editor gazed in awe at the ship-filled room, which looked like the headquarters of the East India Company in 1855, and ordered the maimed journalist to return to head office immediately, where he was disciplined by having to report weddings and funerals.

It's a good example of the need to *appear* busy. Had he been content to keep his miniature fleet out of sight my friend could have had a sinecure for life. If he wanted to work on them he should have gone home (Law Eleven: Being out of the office counts as busy). The great Dr Samuel Johnson once said: 'When solitary be not idle; when idle be not solitary', and I would amend this to read: 'When at your desk be not idle; when idle be not at your desk.'

But this does not mean that the COP actually has to work. Always keep handy some papers to pore over. The person who reads *Lady Chatterley's Lover*, and declaims the more interesting bits aloud for the benefit of colleagues, gets found out. The man with a book underneath the *Financial Times* will survive. Indeed, the *Financial Times* is really an excellent publication and I wish I could afford it. The publishers have made it so big it will hide the average office worker completely, although if sleeping behind it be careful. I knew an old chap who went to sleep every afternoon after lunch behind the *FT* in the belief that people would think he was reading it, but he never realized it was upside down. The more modern version of this wheeze is to go into a trance in front of a desktop computer. Perhaps one day they will design a computer you can hide behind.

Part of the technique of appearing busy is not to get through work too quickly. No credit is given for swift working. Either one is suspected of being slipshod or they simply pile more on. The system is designed to favour the slow, painstaking and stupid.

Be highly mobile. Move rapidly around the building carrying something businesslike about your person – a floppy disk, a ledger or a file.

It is helpful to have a permanent crisis which can be

65

Always keep handy some papers to pore over

produced when necessary as a cover-up or an excuse. An equipment failure is always useful. 'Sheila won't be back for some time. She's seeing the man about the copier. It's on the blink again.' Or, 'John's busy. His VDU is playing up and he's had to borrow one in another room.'

At administrative level the crisis can be more tangible. 'He's gone to see the suppliers about the new desks. They still can't get what we want.' Or perhaps, 'I'm sorry, I have been terribly tied up with the new works at Milton Keynes. The roof keeps collapsing.'

I knew a man who was always 'having trouble' with the stationery store. He felt duty bound to visit them four times a day about the wrong envelopes or the carbon paper. As they were fifteen floors away this took up most of his time. But he overdid it. Colleagues started using the phrase, 'I'm going to the stationery department' as a catchword when they visited the washroom or went to lunch. So crises should gradually be solved and replaced by new ones.

A phone call from senior staff gives a great chance to appear snowed under with toil. My friend Askew used to snap a pair of scissors into the phone to make it sound as if he was typing with one hand while taking the call. He also conducted a sort of broadcast drama, asking the caller to hold on and shouting imaginary messages across the room – 'Just a minute, Joe, let me see that before it goes to Mr Thompson . . . . Here you are, Fred, rush that to Mr Fleming . . . . Jenny, get out the Arkwright file, will you? . . . . Sorry about that, we're rushed off our feet . . . .' Meanwhile the rest of the staff simply ignored him. It looked very strange, poor Askew bellowing across the room and everyone sitting there in silence.

The physical appearance of the desk is vital.

There are two schools of thought about this. The current mode among highly placed executives is to have a completely clear desktop, in line with Henry Ford's maxim that he could tell what a man was like from the top of his desk, meaning if it was cluttered he would fire him. In some esoteric industries such as public relations or advertising the desk for senior management has vanished completely, and is replaced by a glass-topped table with a sofa beside it. This, however, can only succeed if the desk's owner is sufficiently senior to hand out all the chores to others. It's easy to have a clear working surface when all routine work is given to a secretary.

Assuming most COPs will not have reached that level, it is probably best to go to the other extreme. Fill the desk with the apparatus of hard work such as pencil sharpeners, pen racks, dictionaries, timetables, notebooks, calculators and so forth. Also a few copies of business magazines. Have at least one unique piece of office machinery, preferably some Japanese electronic gadget such as a pocket typewriter or mini-computer. Defend the appearance of the desk against the 'clean-top' brigade by stating firmly: 'Henry Ford said, "An empty desk is an empty mind." ' (He said nothing of the sort, but nobody will know.)

If the desk is by a wall, fix a cork-faced notice board there which can be used to advertise the owner's love of toil. It should contain newspaper cuttings, an airline calendar, a letter from someone thanking you, and an Olympic Games poster for 1975. Various important phone numbers can be pinned up, e.g. Ministry of Defence, Euston Station, Russian Embassy etc. Put up imaginary reminders – 'Get monthly figures'; 'See Ministry re planning permission'; 'Town Hall?'; 'Tell J.B. not to bother with A.R. as F.W. has spoken to G.K.'

Special clothes should hang on a hook by the desk, items such as a safety helmet, orange overalls and rubber boots. These are for visiting the site. *It doesn't matter if you don't have a site.* I knew a chap in an insurance office in the City who hung up a collection of outdoor clothes and everyone was most impressed. 'At any minute I might get an urgent call to visit a client on a building site,' he used to explain. 'You've got to be prepared for anything in this job.' For a long time he kept a spade in the corner, 'For digging out the car on site,' he said, mysteriously.

Such wheezes will help the COP in the office, but what about when absent? The answer is to leave behind a large desk diary, open at the appropriate page, as a Silent Sentinel, telling snoopers how hard its owner is working. This is just as important for senior staff as for junior ones. It doesn't help the image for a secretary to say, 'Well, there's nothing in his diary.' The diary should not bear any relation to reality. In fact a genuine diary would merely give an unfortunate impression, since an average day would look like this:

10.00	Cancel visit to works
10–11.00	Coffee
11.00	Ring Jane re dinner tomorrow. Get flowers
1.00	Lunch with Fred. Book table for Thursday
2.30	Sauna
3.00	Ironmongers re rowing machine.
3.45	Haircut
4.45	Pick up Mary from station
MEM:	Do expenses (get fake bill from Baker's Arms): Buy corkscrew: Check Amsterdam night clubs for next week: Sandy's birthday: Ring garage

Scrawled across the page in heavy pencil is some damning memo such as

GET CONTRACEPTIVES FOR SALES CONFERENCE.

Any senior staff reading this will have an impression of idleness and parasitism (the correct impression, in fact). No, the real diary should be hidden away and Silent Sentinel substituted. A typical page in the Silent Sentinel will read:

8.00	On site [you won't get there until 10.00 but it looks good]
11.30	Return from site. Conference
12.30	Wait in over lunch for call from Karachi

1.30   Ring Polytechnic re classes in office management
2.00   Jackson calls
2.30   ICI representative
3.15   Get figures re ML405 and ML406. Note: Is ML405 possible replacement for KB765?
4.00   Let J.B. have report
5.00   See Benskin
6.30   Social club sub-committee
MEM: Get present for old Mrs Wright on way home (90th birthday). Buy pep pills for sales conference. Work on illuminated scroll for presentation to Mr Fosdyke. Start collecting for Christmas gift to Mr Fosdyke. Oxfam box. Buy timetable and *Ways to Improve Your Mind*

The image portrayed by this gibberish is that of a desperately hard-working employee, frequently out of the office, anxious to improve his business knowledge, taking an active part in the running of the firm and generous and kind-hearted to a fault.

Remember, though, that the boss may have different ideas of what constitutes something virtuous. I know at least one miserable man who refuses to contribute to charity on the grounds that helping starving people upsets the ecological balance of the world. He regards the office collector as a sentimental ninny. So adjust entries to the character of people likely to read them – perhaps 'Burn down Red Cross headquarters' or 'Evict old lady.'

Note the ubiquitous phrase ON SITE. As an all-purpose Coarse excuse there is nothing better. Like all the best wheezes it is difficult to check. The other items are deliberately vague. Who knows whether the man from ICI is due to call? Certainly nobody will know whether the social sub-committee meet that evening. Who is the mysterious Mr Jackson? Be careful, though, not to invent a person or organization. In case of illness your replacement might try to fulfil the imaginary arrangements. For years Askew used a mysterious Mr Guggenheim to fill up his diary. When ill he was phoned from the office by a man who asked how could he contact Guggenheim, together with various fictitious firms. 'I can't find XYZ Electronics in the phone book,' he said. 'Do you know the number?'

When Askew said Guggenheim had left the country the man went remorselessly through all the other fake names. It was so distressing Askew had to return to the office next day to avoid having his cover blown. So, while the engagement may be fictitious, let the name be real.

Never have a blank day in the diary. To the managerial mind a blank day means no work. If necessary put in some all-embracing phrase such as 'At site all day' or 'Get filing up to date.' And make sure the diary itself is suitable – not Playboy or the Girl Guides. Preferably use a diary from your best suppliers, which will inevitably be ICI.

Another important item of desk equipment is the tea or coffee cup. This should be of outstanding appearance to attract the eye; it must have the owner's name, initials or nickname painted on; and there must be something to inspire curiosity, a monogram or impressive inscription. This will give the opportunity, when questioned, to say it was presented by the rest of the management course at the Kuala Lumpur Business School or whatever sounds most impressive. Perhaps, 'My old boss gave it to me just before he died.'

Office workers become obsessional about cups. I've known people not speak for weeks because someone used the wrong one. My old boss kept his chained to the desk. It was a souvenir of the time Aston Villa won the FA Cup and he treasured it beyond all earthly goods. One day his secretary broke it when unchained for cleaning and scoured London for a duplicate in vain. The office crisis when he found out was far greater than the time the building caught fire.

Job Title

It is essential for the COP's job to have a dignified title. It may not be possible to rise by promotion, but it *is* possible to do so by having the job renamed. The annual job appraisal gives an opportunity. Let the post clerk become mail executive, the switchboard operator a communications coordinator and the secretaries personal support executives.

The growth of euphemisms has become so rapid that some jobs are now unrecognizable. There used to be lots of men, like my Uncle Walter, who went round with suitcases trying to persuade people to buy their firm's products. For a hundred years they were known as commercial travellers (Dickens once wrote a short story called 'The Uncommercial Traveller'). About thirty years ago they became sales representatives or sales engineers; now they are sales executives or even New Business Executives. The job is the same – only the suitcase has changed.

Years ago I worked with a man who was thick. When our firm folded he couldn't get another newspaper job and had to take a post with an engineering firm as what they called a publicity officer, which meant he sat in a little office and cut bits out of newspapers. But while his former colleagues remained mere office fodder he rose; soon he was called a public relations officer. The last time I saw him he had graduated to head of corporate affairs. He is still thick but now he is wealthy as well.

A title to avoid, however, is senior sales representative. It is usually reserved for worn-out old reps who never made it to managerial status, the sort who boast they've been on the road man and beast for forty years. Another handle to dodge is anything with assistant in it, especially personal assistant, with its suggestion of running errands and making phone calls. I think it was the late Alfred Hitchcock who said that the one man who never becomes a film director is the assistant director.

The best way of avoiding the assistant label is to be known as 'reporting to' the head of department. A friend was assistant public relations officer to a small company, and also edited their information sheet. He was a mere nobody until he persuaded them to retitle the job 'executive in charge of company publications reporting to head of corporate affairs'. From that day he was a different man. Basically he was still a little squirt, but now a cheerful, optimistic squirt.

It will help to have a business card printed, displaying the title, e.g.

John Arthur Brown
Mobile Customer Relations Executive*
XYZ Electronics Plc

Be careful to hand over the correct card. Like everyone, I get my wallet filled with other people's, and once handed over the wrong card. I wished to discuss advertising; my host kept trying to talk about a pension scheme. People are so used to non-communication it took ten minutes to find out what was wrong. Furthermore, he said he'd got interested in pensions now and didn't want to know about advertising. When I left he was ringing the man whose card I'd handed in, and asking him to call round and start a pension plan.

Espionage

Office espionage is freely conducted by management. Papers may be checked deliberately or examined while searching for something in the owner's absence, during which incriminating details may be uncovered, not counting a bottle of scotch in the bottom of the filing cabinet. It will not improve life if the

* i.e. sales rep.

departmental chief finds copies of job applications or rude references to himself in the files. A useful precaution against papers being turned over is to leave imaginary and significant documents among them, perhaps a reminder 'See health authority re state of toilets' or 'Can hear sound of J.B. phoning his daughter in Australia again.' If the COP feels he needs sympathy, why not leave a note for the snooper to find saying, 'Ring migraine clinic for appointment. My God, nobody knows what I am going through. No wonder my work has suffered recently.' To leave a message in a drawer marked private is the best way of spreading information round the office quickly.

Other snooping methods range from the half-open door to the intercom. I worked in a department where the boss used to switch the intercom on without speaking to overhear what the staff were saying, but they could tell when it became live and used to conduct a conversation for his benefit. A typical one went like this:

'Do you like it here, Charlie?'

'It's not so bad but they're offering another twenty quid a week down the road.'

'You wouldn't go, would you?'

'I might. I need the money for my old mother and my three crippled children to buy them a wheelchair each. Because we can't afford three wheelchairs they have to go round strapped to my wife's back. It's difficult going round Sainsbury's with three crippled children tied to your back.'

These outrageous stories, which got wilder and wilder as time went on, usually finished with a sycophantic reference to the boss, such as, 'The only thing that keeps me here is because Mr Wilson is so kind. It isn't his fault the wages are terrible.'

Unfortunately, there was a violent Glaswegian called Angus in the department, and returning, drunk as usual, from lunch he seized the speaker from the table and neatly drop-kicked it against the wall where it shattered into pieces. When asked for an explanation by the manager he said grimly, 'It fell on mah foot.' The manager took the hint and the system was abandoned. Yet life was less interesting without it.

I remember when working on a local newspaper how we cured the editor of his unpleasant habit of opening all correspondence, no matter to whom it was addressed. He would come into the reporters' room, hand over a torn-open envelope and remark on its contents: 'Glad to see your mother is feeling better again' or some such comment. A fake letter was carefully compiled by the staff and addressed to one of them at the office. It was supposed to be from his father and went something like this:

Dear Son,

I am glad to hear you are well and are managing to survive despite the pitiful wages you have to exist on. It must be awful to work for a man who is a byword in the town for meanness and rapacity. I find it difficult to believe that even he would open personal correspondence, as you say.

Did you know, by the way, that you might prosecute him for this? I was talking to your Uncle Fred last night and he was saying he would undertake the case. That is an advantage of having one of the country's finest solicitors in the family! From what you say I think this man is already in contravention of the Factories Act.

Your loving father

We knew the wheeze worked because when he delivered the letter (opened) the editor asked anxiously about the recipient's uncle, was he a good solicitor, etc. etc. He was also heard to ask about the Factories Act.

Since surveillance tactics are adopted by management I see no reason why Coarse Office Persons should not use the same methods themselves. Never neglect the golden hours of lunch or early evening, when the office is deserted, to examine files, letters, spikes and even wastepaper baskets. Vital matters essential to survival may be revealed, like the note turned up by my friend Hicks, which said, 'Hicks is proving very lazy. Can I see you about him?'

Often employers have been aghast at my intimate knowledge of office affairs. A snoop one lunchtime, when I worked in Mayfair, revealed that my chief was charging taxi fares for a journey he made with me on the bus every week. I was also getting paid less than the man who sat opposite. There was a note from a senior executive praising something I had done. It had never been shown to me, doubtless because I might want more money.

Since I took up authorship there is not a publisher in London who dare leave me alone in his office, not since I quickly ran through the correspondence of the editorial director of a large firm and made a note of the advances paid to other authors (a jealously guarded trade secret). Within hours the facts had been broadcast to the publishing world, including the pitiful advance to a penniless elderly writer for a reissue of a major work.

If one is exceptionally lucky, the search will turn up some exciting piece of private information, perhaps a note from an executive's secretary saying she will meet him after going to the family planning clinic.

Develop the ability to read writing upside down. Senior management have an unpleasant habit of discussing something that has arisen from a letter in front of them which they won't allow you to see. Or perhaps it's a confidential report. To make matters worse they just read out selected bits with their heads looking downwards, so all the unhappy victim can hear is, 'It says here that despite their letters you made no effort to . . . mumble . . . mumble . . . don't want that bit, that refers to the chairman . . . rude . . . mumble . . . swore on telephone . . . mumble . . . mumble . . . disgrace . . . mumble . . . yours faithfully . . . mumble . . . .' Now then, what the hell have you

Develop the ability to read writing upside down

got to say about that, eh?' Resist the temptation to reply, 'You can't even read.' Instead learn to read upside down, so that you know the contents as well as the man behind the desk. Practise during the lunch hour by placing a letter on your own desk and trying to read it upside down from six feet away. In this way, you will not only be able to follow the allegations but can learn the bits he won't read out.

Askew became so used to this technique that when his boss called him in and slammed a letter down on the desk right way up, he automatically walked round to the boss's side and read it upside down.

Qualifications

I have always been suspicious of so-called business qualifications since I did a postgraduate certificate of education with students learning to teach business studies. Every single one of them was there because they couldn't make a living at business. While it's true that some teachers have gone into education as a refuge from real life, it does seem ominous that how to be a success is being taught by men who've failed. Worse, their instructors were there because they'd failed too. I remember one student, as part of the course, delivering a test lecture. His subject was 'Projecting Your Image'. Within twenty minutes he had reduced half the class to a deep sleep, broken only when he knocked his flipboard to the ground.

Yet qualifications are still highly regarded and every COP should have one, or even two. But remember: A USELESS QUALIFICATION IS BETTER THAN A GENUINE ONE.

Let me explain. A qualification worth anything, such as a university diploma or degree, requires very hard work. I speak from experience as I took an Open University degree in my forties and tottered forth some years later with an upper second honours, a wiser and better man in every way except for the fact that I had ruined my eyes and digestion and spent all my savings. But a genuine qualification takes up so much time and energy that by the time the student's got it he's been overtaken in the office race. While I was studying, other writers' work filled the bookshops; *Punch* implored me to write in vain; the BBC went down on their knees for something. All to no avail as I plodded through Weber's analysis of bureaucratic structure.

When I returned, clutching my degree, nobody wished to know. True, I could quote Weber, Durkheim, Skinner, Wordsworth, Dickens, T.S. Eliot, Ptolemy and Copernicus at the drop of a hat; but that's not much help when everyone's forgotten you. Worse happened to another chap on the course. He took the degree with the idea of getting promotion. By the time he'd graduated his former secretary had become his boss. The fact that he asked her to address him as BA on all memos was small consolation.

There are so many qualifications around these days that they mean the same to most employers. Even hairdressers put letters after their names. Besides, employers are suspicious of qualifications which seem *too* good. Many an Open University student has returned from summer school saying, 'Personally it all seems rather unnecessary to me, all this rushing around trying to sell baked beans. There must be more to life than that.' Views of that sort are dangerous in the sales department. The best qualification is something genuine but useless, obtained without study and impressive. In this respect nothing beats membership of a so-called professional body. There are no examinations, or only such as a buffoon could pass, and the resulting letters look far more meaningful than a mere BA. How much better is MISEHI (Member of the Institute of Sales Executives in the Heating Industry). Or MIAT (Member of the Institute of Advanced Typing). Those are imaginary, but there are plenty of real ones just as good. Be careful, though, not to try to join a serious professional body such as the Royal College of Surgeons or the Pharmaceutical Society. The

79

exams are rather difficult. Choose one of the many kangaroo institutions.

Having obtained the 'qualification', use it. Have the letters after your name. Write an article for the institute magazine (they're so desperate they'll take any rubbish) and paste up the cutting prominently. Quote from it freely. Ask for time off to attend the annual meeting and conferences. If they have a badge or tie, wear it.

A man who used to live near me always referred to his trade organization as 'The learned body I belong to'. It was in reality little more than a collection of cowboy engineers. He volunteered to 'design' new lighting for the local church hall and this was gladly accepted. I suppose the design was all right but we never found out because it was impossible to switch on all the lights at once. The first time this was done there was a series of explosions and, as we couldn't afford to have it all done again, nowadays we just hold the Scout meetings in semi-darkness.

A special skill such as shorthand or double-entry book-keeping is always impressive. In default of the real thing invent your own. Most secretaries invent their own shorthand in any case. Make strange signs on the paper and explain it's a cross between Pitman and Greig. But be careful not to be landed in a difficult situation. When I was a young reporter my notebook was ordered to be produced as evidence in a defamation case. With great embarrassment I explained to the judge that it would be incomprehensible to anyone but myself. The judge insisted on examining it, however, and eventually found a word that looked like pig.

'Did you call the plaintiff a pig?' he asked the defendant.
'No, my lord.'
'It says here you did.'

At this point I had to explain that 'pig' was my private contraction for 'town councillor'. There were lots more, such as 'pox' for the Borough Surveyor and 'scum' for the Deputy

Town Clerk, but the judge admitted defeat and returned the book with a severe glance.

Finally, a human wheeze which will smooth the office path. Be responsible for donating something to the office community, whether it's a picture or a new teapot. There is at this moment a man with a well-paid job in Brook Street, Mayfair, who was due to be made redundant five years ago but on the eve of the blow falling donated to the office a new coffee-making machine of Swedish design. But never give something controversial. My cousin, who was keen on art, gave his office a rather unusual picture by a minor French painter of the twenties. It was quite valuable, but somewhat obscene. The cleaner refused to dust it ('Filth, I call it') and the boss was overheard to say, 'I'm a bit worried about Johnson. He seems obsessed by sex. He's hung a dirty picture over his desk.' Finally he had to take it down and it was replaced by a Pirelli calendar.

6

Promotion and Responsibility

For promotion cometh neither from the east, nor from the west;
Nor yet from the south.
Book of Common Prayer

It might be thought that a COP would never receive promotion, but this is not so. As long as one doesn't actually commit a crime, promotion is almost certain to come; lack of interest or ability is not necessarily a bar. Indeed, it seems a recommendation in some places. This chapter, therefore, deals with the special problems that come with responsibility, for COP's are found at all levels of office life from the low to the high; they are not confined to hewers of wood and drawers of water. It's just the trimmings that are different as one goes higher up.

The first task every day of a promoted COP is to make a list of things to do. Not that he or she need do them. That is not management's job. What's the point of being promoted otherwise? They are for other people. This should be placed prominently on the desk and the first entry must be 'Make list'. Then follow such items as:

Arrangements for conference
Organization chart
See R.P.
Get last Friday's *FT*
Smith funeral
British Leyland

These jobs are then handed out to staff: 'Can you get me that organization chart, Betty? . . . John, will you get on to R.P., please? . . . Sheila, ring the *FT* and ask for a copy of last Friday's issue with the article on cement . . . . Betty, order a wreath for Smithy's funeral and put on the card, 'To a dear old friend from his heartbroken colleagues'. . . . Jack, when are we going to hear from British Leyland?' All this should be done within ten minutes of arrival. Thus an impression of bustle, activity and command is created in the first part of the day, and with luck it will last for the other six hours and fifty minutes. Exhausted by telling everybody what to do, the COP has hardly strength to totter forth to a 'working' lunch and fill in a breakdown of his time at the end of the day. Do not attempt to break the hallowed tradition of British management and do anything yourself. It will bring the most serious rebuke known to higher management: 'Why on earth don't you get your secretary to do that, old chap?'

In fact the only actual work to be done is trying to contact senior management. This in itself can be a full-time job, the ratio being one hour of waiting and prowling for every thirty seconds of actual conversation. Incredible measures are needed. My friend Peter Hicks says he used to travel up and down in the lift all day until he caught the marketing director and then pounced on him. Prowling around outside an executive's office is an uncertain method, as by some mischance two may come out together, deep in conversation, and you've wasted your time. I have known quite senior staff reduced to waiting on the pavement to snatch a word as the wanted man steps into his car. If management should accidentally flit by, seize them immediately whether you have anything to say or not. The chance to talk may not occur again.

The most important thing to avoid, when promoted, is innovation. New and creative thinking is not wanted. When top management think an overhaul is needed they prefer to bring in outside consultants and pay them the earth rather than accept ideas from within. A person who puts up an imaginative and useful idea will be met with the full flood of senior disapproval. Take the case of a man who became public relations officer to a small airline. Just before one board meeting he deliberately made the room filthy, with coffee spilt on the tables and carpets, cigarette ends all over the place and what looked like a heap of vomit on the floor. The board entered and looked in horror.

'There you are gentlemen,' cried the PRO. 'Now you really know how unpleasant it is to wait in our departure lounge and why we are losing passengers so rapidly.'

If he expected a chorus of praise he was mistaken. They looked at him as if he was insane and then asked him to get the mess cleared up so they could start work. 'In any case, the state of the departure lounge isn't your department,' said the chairman. He didn't last very long.

So expect no reward for a bright idea, whether it's making the managing director man the switchboard so he really knows what's going on or holding conferences standing up so that they finish more quickly.

It may help to remember the traditional stages of any useful office project:

1. Enthusiasm
2. Doubt
3. Disillusionment
4. Panic
5. Search for a scapegoat
6. Punish the innocent
7. Reward the guilty

While sensible innovation is frowned upon, crazy ideas are acceptable and much approved of, *provided they come from America, Japan or out of a book written by an idiot*. A good example is hot desking. This is an innovation from the States whereby there are fewer desks in a department than people, forcing them to keep on the road, where presumably their duty lies. While

Hot desking

the practical effect of this is that staff are reduced to writing sales reports standing up against a wall or typing letters on the floor, it is considered an example of enlightened management. Why not invent similar outrageous wheezes and put them forward as genuine improvements? For instance:

Electric toileting: To stop employees spending too much time in the washrooms the number of cubicles in each toilet is reduced to one, stimulating self-control and reducing cleaning costs.

Cooperative typing: Everybody uses one typewriter. This cuts down paperwork as nobody can get anything typed.

Zero seating: Abolish all chairs. Employees must work standing up. (Since writing that I have found this is taken seriously now. The theory says best use of space is made by having a ledge round the wall with people standing at it.)

The negative door: Remove all doors. The drop in temperature will stimulate hard work. Lack of doors will facilitate easy movement from department to department. Maintenance will be reduced.

These need not actually be put into use. Simply suggest them. 'Of course I suppose we could adopt the new American system of negative doors . . . .' Having made a suggestion with a New York flavour will be enough.

On new ideas I always think of the example quoted by Robert Townsend in *Further Up The Organisation*. When head of the investment department of American Express, he urgently needed a revolutionary new calculator which would create great economies. The purchasing department said he couldn't have it as it wasn't in his budget, so he pulled out his letter of resignation (which Mr Townsend seemed to carry about all the time) and asked the man to sign it. 'If the president should ask why, I'm going to tell him because some stupid son of a bitch in the purchasing department won't buy me a machine that would pay for itself in the first three and a half minutes we owned it,' thundered Mr Townsend. He got the machine.

Brave words, with a nice storybook ending, but in most companies how different. To start with, the man from purchasing would not sign the resignation but would try to add it up. The president (i.e. chairman) would ignore it, and call him in for a fatherly chat.

'Now then, Robert, what's all this I hear about you upsetting nice old Mr Perkins in the purchasing department?'

'The goddam idiot refused to let me have . . . .'

'Yes, I know all about that. He was very distressed, you know. Apparently it brought on his asthma again. He had quite a turn after you stormed out. I hope he doesn't complain to his union. We don't want all the clerks out, with the annual audit coming up.'

'But I tell you this calculator would save us millions.'

'I don't doubt it would. If silk purses were sows' ears we should all be rich. Now look, why don't you come out to lunch and forget about it all, eh? If you want to get out the figures more quickly I'll get you another girl.'

(Note the lunch invitation. It is one of the great fallacies of senior management that a free meal solves everything.)

So beware of advice to take courage in both hands and storm in to the boss and tell him what's what. These books never say what happens if the approach doesn't succeed. However, do not take this to mean innovation is impossible. What is needed is the trappings of reorganization, charts on walls, diagrams everywhere, coloured models, a large critical flowpath. Rearrange desks every month. Be in permanent revolution but be careful to ensure that nothing is actually achieved. Draw the attention of senior management to the new look. 'Seen the arrangement of the desks? It increases throughput by 10 per cent.'

Keep the office looking busy, especially if somebody import-ant is likely to pass through. Management are suspicious of the silent office – they think everyone is doing the crossword. A colleague who ran a small advertising agency actually borrowed ten people from outside to make the office look busy when an important client called. He got five from the firm next door, four from the pub and one total stranger. They were all very impressive, rushing around with folders of drawings and phoning all over the place. The only one who let him down was the man from the office next door, who overdid the act, clawing his temples and crying, 'My God, can't anybody ever get anything right in this place?'

'You seem very busy,' said the visitor. 'Will you have time to do my order?'

Reports

Just as lower management have to justify their position, so do senior management, and one of the easiest ways to achieve this is making futile alterations in any report submitted to them. Make their task and yours as simple as possible by giving room to manoeuvre. Why not leave out a complete section, having prepared the material and put it by? This will give management a chance to feel clever at having spotted the missing section. Unfortunately, while senior executives have a habit of tinkering with detail in a report, they frequently miss monumental errors, and may fail to notice a vital paragraph has been omitted. In that case, insert it on redrafting.

Submit reports as late as possible. If they are put in too early it suggests that not enough work was done and it leaves too much time for fiddling alterations. Friday evening is a good time. It gives an executive an excuse to say he's worked over the weekend ('I looked at your report down in Hampshire. My God, I wish I worked union hours'). The truth is it got a cursory glance between gins, but pretend to be impressed.

Reports should contain as much meaningless buffoon-type business jargon as possible. Avoid direct phrases such as 'This is rubbish.' Above all, avoid any literary quality or anything which suggests you belong to the same race as Milton and Shakespeare. I remember once putting in a report which said: 'It seems to me we must be "bloody, bold and resolute", to quote *Macbeth*.' I received it back with a comment scribbled across: 'Who is this Mac Beth? Is he a Scottish representative? Tell him I don't approve of his language.'

As regards the use of jargon, most of it is so ridiculous it's possible to make up your own. For a joke, a consultant friend invented a term in an article for a business magazine: 'this policy,' he wrote, 'must eventually lead to ongoing *phthisis* of the market share.' (Phthisis is an old word for consumption or tuberculosis – a dreadful disease of the sort that Edgar Allan Poe's characters always got.) Over the next few months other writers borrowed the phrase. He finally knew he was successful when it was repeated in the headline of a business publication: 'More Market Phthisis'. Here are a few more suggestions:

The taction factor makes the price attractive.
The product is subject to swage.
There was some boraging of the market.

Many will already be familiar with the Functional Verbal Obscurity Chart, details of which have been published in newspapers and books. It consists of three columns of words, the first two adjectives and the last nouns. To concoct instant impressive jargon, just take a word from each column. Thus:

Adjective	Adjective	Noun
Ongoing	Reciprocal	Mobility
Corporate	Synchronized	Situation
Optional	Monitored	Identity

From this may be concocted 'Ongoing synchronized identity' or 'Optional reciprocal mobility' and other combinations. The situation (sorry, the corporate monitored concept) has now reached a state where some large firms have to provide their own dictionaries so employees can understand the internal jargon or bizspeak.

But there are other ways besides jargon of raising a smokescreen and baffling people either verbally or in writing. Deliberately misunderstanding someone's meaning is one. There is an American director of a London company who, whenever his deputy disagrees with him, nods wisely and says, 'I see you still have a personality problem, Joe.'

'What do you mean, a personality problem?'

'You feel compelled to oppose all decisions by people senior to you.'

'I don't feel compelled to do anything. I just don't agree with you.'

'Of course, Joe. I want you to know we all feel very supportive towards you in your problem. I want you to feel you can always discuss your difficulty and maybe together we shall find a solution.'

Nothing short of a hammer will penetrate a screen of this sort. The friend who described the above conversation eventually surrendered and agreed with everything. The director told him, 'Joe, I have to say how I admire the way you have overcome your disability. Few men would have had the perseverance.'

Trouble and Decisions

Cultivate the skill of not being there when the crime is committed or a decision has to be made. Your seniors will already have developed it to a fine degree. When I was a young lad I worked in an office where the boss never went to lunch until the unfashionable hour of 2.15 p.m. I asked why he chose such an inconvenient time.

'So he won't have to make a decision, of course,' came the reply. It was explained that by going out at 2.15 he avoided the busiest part of the day, when a lot of decisions had to be made. This little wheeze enabled him to blame his subordinates if anything went wrong and had the added advantage of making him appear working when others were resting. He was very fond of leaving messages on desks which began, 'While you were at lunch I discovered that . . . .' So many executives are doing this now that the hour of lunch is becoming later and later. This has the extra bonus for an executive that by the time he's lurched back to the office there's only time to sign some letters before catching the train for Chiselhurst.

A good crime to be absent from is the sack. Coarse People won't have to sack many persons, but those they do will be lower ranks and it's far more difficult to sack someone low down than it is to fire a senior person.

To dismiss the marketing director simply requires a letter from the chairman on these lines:

> My Dear Rodney,
>
> At the last meeting of the board concern was expressed at the hard way you had worked over the last three years and about the state of your health. With sales figures so unsatisfactory we feel we cannot expose you to further immense effort which will be needed to put the company on a steady course [*You idle bastard*]. We have reluctantly, therefore, decided to ask you to step down from your onerous duties and pass the burden to younger, if less well qualified, shoulders [*i.e.* —— *off*]. You will, of course, be paid until your contract expires in two years' time and will receive in addition a terminal grant. I see no reason why you should not keep the car and yacht which you found necessary for entertaining overseas visitors.
>
> Yours etc.

What a charming letter. There is nothing to argue about except perhaps whether he gets the Knightsbridge flat as well.

But things are not so easy for the COP. It may be easy to fire an executive, but it is far from simple to sack a typist, clerk or cleaner.

There is no dignified exchange of letters. Instead . . . .

'Good morning, Mrs Barnaby. Could I have a word with you?'

'And I should like a word with you and all. How much longer are your bleeding staff going to throw their cigarette ends on the bleeding carpet? Haven't they ever heard of bleeding ash-trays?'

'Yes, Mrs Barnaby. Could you turn the Hoover off? Could you turn . . . . Thank you. That's better. I'm afraid I've got bad news for you, Mrs Barnaby. We all think the world of you, but –'

'I should bleeding well hope they did, sweeping up their fag ends night and day . . . .'

'That's just it. Mrs Barnaby. You won't have to sweep up fag ends any more. The board have decided to get the cleaning done by contract, so you . . . . you won't have to come in . . . and we do think the world of you . . . but we do have to think of the office too . . . .'

A blank stare. She is giving no help. Suddenly:

'You filthy bleeder.'

'Now then, Mrs Barnaby, don't be violent.'

'Night and day I work here for fifteen years and I come in that Bank Holiday two years ago after that special conference and they had cigar butts, yes, bleeding cigar butts thrown all over the carpets and the things I found in the lavatories – well, those lavatories could tell a tale or two if they could speak. Just you wait till I tell my husband when he gets back from the coal wharf. He'll bring the whole karate class along with him and do you, Mr Smarty Pants.'

By now the COP is backed up against the wall with the nozzle of a vacuum cleaner stuck in his face. With a final snort Mrs Barnaby pulls out the dust bag and empties it over his desk and stalks forth. The COP collapses at his desk and determines next time to get someone else to do the dirty work.

The Golden Wheeze for lower management is to copy their betters. Always be around for something pleasant, such as a retirement presentation or a birthday; never be seen when there's stormy weather, such as redundancies to be discussed or someone reprimanded. Remember Law 1 of Coarse Office Life: Keep moving.

As well as sacking people, the COP may have to choose staff below him. Be equally careful. Never employ anyone more clever than you as a subordinate. The ideal assistant is simple but uninspired. Otherwise your own job, or even the whole department, may be at risk.

It might help to remember the system of grading officer candidates used in the German Army in World War II. These were listed as: efficient and hard-working; efficient and idle; inefficient and idle; inefficient and hard-working. Those graded efficient and hard-working were recommended for active service posts, those efficient and idle for staff jobs. Even those inefficient and idle were not rejected completely as it was argued that because they were idle their inefficiency wouldn't do much harm and they might be suitable for a minor admin. job. The one class that failed were those who were both inefficient and hard-working, on the grounds that their misplaced energy would do great damage. A point worth remembering: brisk inefficiency is the most terrible quality to have in an assistant.

The most dangerous subordinates are those who point out what is wrong with the organization. I knew someone who took on a young graduate with a mathematics degree. 'Clever lad,' he said. 'He'll be useful with the computer.' Within six months the young genius had proved conclusively that the department was not necessary and that lots of money could be saved by abolishing it. The report was buried, of course, so he went straight to the top and won his point. My friend found himself

Brisk inefficiency is the most terrible quality to have in an assistant

redundant along with the rest of his department, but the mathematical genius now heads an ever-growing department of his own. Most of his staff are computers, tended by one or two human slaves.

Conferences

When in doubt hold a conference.

It is a fairly harmless method of wasting time and can be used as a substitute for leadership and decision. Coarse managers are always holding conferences; and when they aren't holding their own they're attending other people's.

Like expenses, conference-holding is an art form in its own right, with talks or films sandwiched between gin-filled get-togethers. In this respect, the zenith was reached by a sales director who demonstrated to his board that the geographical centre of their sales territory was not London, but Hamburg. 'Why, therefore, are we wasting money on having conferences in London,' he asked, 'when it would be cheaper to have all the European reps assemble in Hamburg?' This novel idea was greeted with acclamation. All members of the board volunteered to take part in the experiment. Next month a planeload of intoxicated sales staff and executives left London. Five hours later they were hard at work in the Reeperbahn watching prostitutes wrestle in mud and pouring steins of beer down their throats.

Alas, though equally useless, few conferences are as merry as that. They are usually held because nobody can think of anything else to do. Nevertheless, it is important to be seen to be active at a conference. But do not think it is an exchange of ideas. Management want confirmation of what they already think, not contradictions. At my brother's first sales conference as rep for an international food firm, they were discussing why sales of one product were so bad. Now we'd been eating that product at home, thanks to Roger's samples, and it was lousy. Even the dog refused it. So my brother took his courage in both hands, stood up and said the sales were bad because the product was no good.

'My mother hates it,' he said. 'My dad won't eat it and my brother tries to give his to the dog.'

There was a terrible silence as if he had blasphemed hideously. Then the sales director rose. 'I hope,' he said in a voice trembling with emotion, 'that we shall have no more of that sort of negative thinking at this conference.' To this there were loud and sycophantic cries of 'Hear, hear' and my brother sat down scarlet with shame, while the others blamed the advertising, the packaging, the promotion, the retailers, the price – everything except the taste.

However, it is important to be seen to make some contribution. The simplest way is to grab the central point of interest, usually the blackboard or an overhead projector. Once there, you can control the meeting. There's no need to say anything very meaningful – write a simple heading on the board, such as MOTIVATION, and ask for comments. Write these on the board and end with a masterly summary, 'So you see we have at least six different views on what people mean by motivation.' This is a useful wheeze if running a conference without any idea of what to say.

To gain attention sit near an attractive female member of the staff or make sure one sits near your seat. It's surprising how often people will glance in that direction. But if you wish to lie low and remain anonymous, steer clear of glamour.

The Canteen

A canteen is not just somewhere to eat, it is the biggest cause of strife in British industry and commerce. There are more strikes over grub than over pay, which is not surprising when the canteen is used as a form of emphasizing rank rather than as a restaurant. When I worked in the steel industry they laid on a Christmas lunch at a Midlands works and charged everybody £2. They then arranged a special meal for senior management, starting with smoked salmon, followed by turkey and washed down with copious draughts of hock, Burgundy and Benedictine. This was free (or rather the shareholders paid for it). When the news leaked out there was a strike and the firm were unable to understand why.

The key to the executive washroom is nothing compared to the privilege of eating in the senior dining room. There is a large firm in Yorkshire which has no fewer than five grades of eating place. In the lowest, men in overalls fall asleep with their heads in a plate of egg and chips; at the highest (or Golden Trough as it is known) they sip sherry and nibble olives before tucking into port and melon.

So eating in the right place is important. People are judged by where they eat. If dissatisfied with your placing, there is only one thing to do: shun the canteen. Be known to avoid it. Ostentatiously eat elsewhere and refuse to meet anyone there. Then get on the canteen committee. This isn't difficult, as people never seem to last for more than one meeting. If from a position on the committee it is not possible to move up a grade of trough, then your case is hopeless.

Useful Excuses

1. That's the way we've always done it
2. If you want to change the system, OK, but . . . .
3. Not my job
4. Why didn't you say you wanted it quickly?
5. Nobody told us anything about it
6. My secretary/assistant/deputy/boy/girl was away
7. Are you quite sure it was me you spoke to?

8. I was on leave at the time
9. I took the papers home and the dog ate them
10. I forgot

7

Expenses, Travel and Perks

> It is better to travel hopefully than to arrive.
> Robert Louis Stevenson

Travel is a great opportunity. The further a COP gets from the office, the less control can be exercised. It is the first duty of every man and woman to get out of the office as much as possible, whether it is a sales trip to Rome or down the road for a sandwich.

The first item that comes to mind when away is, of course, expenses. These have developed into an industry of their own and if the same mental energy was put into production and administration as is put into compiling expense sheets, then this country's economic problems would be solved overnight. In fact there are some offices where professional operators will do colleagues' expenses for a 10 per cent commission, on the lines of the professional village letter writers of old India. Expenses have become a challenge, a matter of personal honour rather than money.

The compulsion to beat the system is extraordinary. As a child, I remember an elderly and distant relative, clerk in an old-fashioned firm, who had to take work home. He used an old steel-nib pen and bottle of ink in traditional style, and one day tried to charge for a new bottle of ink. His request was rejected by the company secretary with contempt. My relative brooded over the years as both he and the company secretary grew older. It was suggested that he should retire, but he wouldn't hear of it; he still sat every day at a high desk, wearing mittens without fingers to keep out the cold. Then one day the company secretary, worn out and old, retired. Immediately Cousin Albert claimed an ink allowance from his successor and, having established the principle, retired himself. He died soon afterwards, a happy man.

His story is common, as common as the cry: 'I'll get that back from the bastards if it's the last thing I do.'

In writing expenses the great error is to be too modest. The successful expense sheet is daring and imaginative. Nothing irritates whoever is passing the expenses more than a cringing, sycophantic, Uriah Heep approach, of which I give a typical example:

Tube fare Holborn to Tottenham Court Road	30p
Coffee and biscuits	60p
VAT	9p
Gratuity	6p
Bus fare Oxford Circus to Piccadilly	20p
Stamps (two letters)	38p
Envelopes	36p
Tip to hotel doorman	20p
New pen	15p

My Uncle Walter always tells of a colleague who was foolish enough to charge lunch for his dog, which had to be taken everywhere with him. Outraged by this, the department chief disallowed nearly everything he claimed. Remember, it takes as long to go through a cringing expenses sheet as a bold one, and a boss will not bless you for wasting his time.

There is no higher art form than a good, red-blooded expenses sheet. It makes the *Mona Lisa* look banal by comparison. The total amount charged has nothing to do with a claim being struck out. Most employees' expenses are trifling compared with those of senior people, who spend more on lunch than their staff do on three meals and a bed. Large expense accounts will be queried because of a *negative approach* which does not reflect achievement. Here is a typical imaginative but negative expenses sheet:

To entertaining various potential customers	£236
Hotel (two nights)	£60
Lunch for contact	£20
Sundries	£15

Even if bills are attached, this will be queried because it does not show any business brought in for the expenses record. And talking of bills, management know perfectly well these can be faked and some unscrupulous operators even print their own. Visiting Askew's house on Sunday evening was like watching *The Times* being produced, with type and ink all over the place and fantastic names being invented (Hotel Splendide, Milton Keynes). 'Very expensive place the old Splendide,' Askew used to mutter as he got out his rubber stamp, 'almost as dear as the Ritz at Goole.'

What is needed is a positive approach. The ideal expense account reflects business done and success achieved (whether in fact any success has been achieved or not). It is a bold man who dares to strike out a claim which refers to a successfully concluded deal. Here is an example of positive thinking:

Date: 11:85*

Negotiations with Arkwright team re project 892/MZ/786 (five sessions): Subsistence, meals etc.	£237.50
(see letter of intent ref 56/85)	
Lunch for chairman of Arkwright's on completion of negotiations	£35.00
Return fare to Wolverhampton to deliver contract by hand	£25.00

* Add the date. You might get away with it.

Lunch	£10.70
Taxi	£5.15

To entertaining Webster's representatives re Cairo project (see letter of enquiry 5/10/85)	£35.00

Here is an expense account that reflects a life of endless toil spent gaining contracts, travelling to Wolverhampton and talking to senior people. As with all the best claims, much of it is unverifiable. But remember not to charge for high living. Glamorous expense sheets ('Visit to night club with customers . . . £100') may be queried by some jealous underling cooped up all day in the accounts department. Try to make every item appear not only mundane but full of suffering and toil. Put a night club visit down to hiring a hall to deliver a sales talk. Note that the contract, because of its importance, was delivered by hand. Keep mobile.

As I have said, the best expenses cannot be checked. The palm in this direction goes to a colleague in India who charged for accommodation and when asked for the bill said he stayed with an illiterate (but expensive) peasant. Pressed for some sort of evidence he produced a block of wood with '5000 rupees' carved on it. He is closely followed by another master of the art who alleged he travelled 400 miles to the Congo Basin by taxi. 'I couldn't get a train,' he said. 'There's no railway.'

It is a good idea occasionally to lure the accounts department into a trap, tempt them to challenge an item and then dramatically prove them wrong. This will make them wary of future challenges. I am thinking of my friend Hicks, who once solemnly charged for a rubber dinghy with outboard motor to visit a remote Scottish island. When this was queried he carried the huge object into the office and plonked it on the chief accountant's desk. 'Will you please accept this,' he said, 'otherwise I shall have to charge storage.' Another pal, who sold life insurance, took his kids to lunch on the firm and the bill

As with all the best claims, much of it is unverifiable

specified two half-portions. When the accounts department triumphantly accused him of entertaining his children, he replied that the guests were two jockeys interested in a pension scheme.

Ensure that colleagues don't cut across your territory. At a recent Cup Final no fewer than five people in a City firm charged for taking a client to the game, together with wining and dining him. Unfortunately they all named the same person and received an acid note asking how this gentleman was supposed to have eaten five lunches, all in different restaurants, and consumed eight bottles of wine.

I was once a victim of this procedure myself. An impecunious friend, trying to support a wife, family and mistress, was reduced to inventing lunches with contributors to the magazine he edited and tended to use my name frequently. ('To entertaining Michael Green, author and *Sunday Times* writer, to discuss feature on London at night . . . £44'). I used to feel a bit peeved at this because I never so much as saw a glass of water, but worse was to follow because the editor's boss, angry at his expenses, banned me from writing for the magazine.

'I don't want any more articles from this chap Green,' he snarled. 'He's too damn expensive. If he thinks he can lunch at the Savoy every time he writes a piffling little piece, then he's mistaken.'

Sometimes a genuine expense will be incurred in the line of duty which is refused by the firm. These may range from spilling curry all over your trousers while entertaining a customer to losing luggage at the airport. Firms are funny over this. While they will cheerfully fork out £200 for hiring a car they baulk at paying £25 to replace some trousers. It is the accountancy mind. If this happens, never meet them head-on. Avoid a direct clash. Patience is the hallmark of the master expense operator. Get back the money in little extras over the months. The ability to disguise one expense as another is essential for success. There was a New York theatre critic forty years ago who always wore an expensive opera cloak to first nights. Once, there was a fire at the theatre and his cloak was lost in the confusion. His claim for a new one was rejected by the management. He took this calmly; he said nothing, but when he submitted his expenses the following month he took them in personally to the accountant and waved them in his face. 'I defy you to find the opera cloak,' he growled. They were unable to do so.

To end this section, here is a true story of How to Mismanage Expenses. It concerns a departmental chief who took a day off to attend the funeral of one of his colleagues ('Well, it's not worth coming in before lunch'), and then had the audacity to charge the wreath on his expenses. The item was passed since he signed his own expenses, but it was noted in the accounts department and for months afterwards he was known as The Man Who Charged Bert Jenkins' Wreath on His Exes. People went around staring at him. In the end he was so unpopular he got another job. Not that Bert would have minded. My recollection of him was as a Master Craftsman and it would have given him great pleasure to know that his grave was being decorated at the expense of the firm.

Status Symbols

I have never been able to understand the obsession with the car as an extension of the male ego, but it is true that the average person would die rather than have a less expensive car than some rival. Even my old Uncle Walter used to say, 'I would pass away happy, my boy, if they would only exchange my Ford Popular for a Morris Minor.' The COP should avoid the struggle, remarking that love of powerful cars is usually associated with sexual impotence. In any case cars are old hat. The helicopter is the new status symbol: the dormitory of the super-rich, the little village of Preston Candover in Hampshire, is supposed to have more helicopters per head of the population than anywhere else in the country.

Status symbols change so rapidly these days that it may be more advantageous to opt out of the race. Secretaries as a symbol, for instance, have given way to private computers, some of them programmed to fulfil the emotional and support-ive role of a secretary, with the voice synthesizer crooning, 'You are wonderful, sir' and other flattering phrases soothing to the managerial ear.

Any chosen symbol should therefore be timeless. Remember that only twenty years ago the electronic calculator was regarded as the peak of status. Now they give them away. So pick something that won't date, perhaps a grandfather clock, an antique desk, or something completely outrageous such as a steam alarm clock. One colleague, on promotion, bought in a junk shop a huge nineteenth-century piece of apparatus called a Gasogene, a primitive form of soda syphon consisting of two vast glass globes one on top of the other. Soda was produced by chemical action and the process was as dramatic as an eruption by Mount Etna. Visitors were awestruck and failed to notice that he had to share a secretary.

Travel

I make no apology for repeating that in Coarse Office Life it is best to keep on the move and this applies not merely to senior staff jetting round the world, but to the typist always hopping out for a sandwich ('Hunger pains' is a good excuse, or 'I've got a young ulcer'). Who can do anything to an absent person except leave a peremptory note (which you never received – it must have blown on to the floor).

The mistake many people make is to become so intoxicated with escaping that they mix pleasure with business to a reckless degree. Again it is true at all levels, from the sales director unconscious in a Singapore night club to the typist who, having finished her sandwich, slips into the cinema. There seems some Supernatural Law which says that if you overdo it you get punished. My worst experience of being punished was on an assignment to Paris. Overjoyed at being released from the office I celebrated so dramatically at the airport I was too ill to get on the plane and had to return home.

Take my friend Hicks. He thought he was being clever in travelling from London to Hamburg via Athens at the firm's expense, so he could see his Greek girlfriend. But there was fog at Athens and he eventually arrived in Hamburg thirty minutes before he was due to deliver a two-hour speech to a big conference. 'It was not a success,' he said. 'There was no time to change and my tie had been snipped off in a Greek night club. I had to wear a scarf and pretend I had a sore throat. I'd brought the wrong speech and there wasn't time to prepare another, so I had to use that, and it didn't make sense to them as it was meant to be delivered to British farmers, not German manufacturers. Also I kept falling asleep as I spoke. I think a French firm got the contract.'

Here is another cautionary tale against greed. A vice-president of an American air conditioning firm used to make frequent trips from Florida to Japan. Then an airline started offering vouchers for free holidays on completion of so many trips. This airline didn't have a direct route to Japan but, undeterred, the greedy executive switched to it and travelled via Boston and Anchorage. Six months later an exhausted, grey-faced individual staggered into the airline clutching a sheaf of old tickets to claim his free holiday in Honolulu. The day after he arrived there he collapsed. The doctor said it was due to stress and strain. When he returned to his office there had been a reorganization 'and we're afraid you don't fit into the new pattern, Frank'.

It is tempting, if on a fixed travel allowance, to make money by living cheap abroad. Beware. This led to my being rudely

107

awakened at 3 a.m. in a cheap hotel near the Gare du Nord in Paris, and lined up in the lobby with thirty Algerians, most of them wanted for something unpleasant. A friend had an even more alarming experience in Tokyo. He decided to save by staying at a genuine Japanese hotel instead of the plastic international variety. They spoke no English at Reception but by signs he indicated what he wanted and was shown a room. After a few minutes a girl appeared and started bowing and hissing at him. Every time she hissed, he hissed back. This seemed to excite her, so she hissed even more and he hissed back even more. Suddenly, with a wild shriek, she started to claw off his trousers. This was the start of a series of misunderstandings which ended with him standing on the bed fending off the girl with a hairbrush. Apparently he had booked into a house of ill-fame by mistake. A man who spoke English came to the rescue and said he had inadvertently ordered every special service on the list. Every hiss was another item. 'Not for nothing is this place known as the Inn of the Sixty-nine Happinesses,' he said.

The Business Lunch

One of the more unusual facets of any office is that senior staff are incapable of discussing anything unless intoxicated with alcohol and stupefied with food (that also applies to parts of the public sector). Like expenses, a business lunch has become an art form in its own right and any relation to business or lunch has long since disappeared. In fact the whole concept is now being extended with the working breakfast, which enables everybody to be thoroughly bloated by nine o'clock.

Its magnetism is astonishing, as I found when acting as public relations consultant to an engineering company. I happen to be rather fond of old steamboats, and when I found one rotting away in a yard near the Thames I suggested to the company that they restore it, paint it in company colours and steam it up and down the river. They told me I was crazy. 'Can't you think of a better way of wasting money?' sneered the managing director.

I then had inspiration. I suggested to the board they could use the boat to entertain important customers. 'You could all have lunch while steaming up the Thames,' I said.

At the magic word 'lunch' their piggy snouts twitched. 'Michael,' said the MD, 'I think you have hit upon something. I suppose you can put a fridge for white wine on a steamboat?' Their first trip lasted three hours and the noise was heard at Kew Bridge. Most of them had to be helped ashore, except for one foreign customer who had to be carried. The boat has now been nicknamed *The Ship that Died of Shame* and is in danger of sinking under the weight of claret carried.

That's why I became very worried when I read that the Prime Minister had a working lunch with the German Chancellor. If it's anything like the average working lunch they'd finish up lolling in their chairs and grinning at each other and saying something like, 'I tell you what, let's drop a ——ing atom bomb on the whole lot.'

So Law 73 of Coarse Office Life is: Never discuss business at a business lunch. Never discuss work at a working lunch. Unless, of course, you don't care what decisions are reached. The idea that seemed so wonderful with a bottle of Beaune inside you may look less attractive next morning. One reason why publishers are always going bankrupt is that they can't talk about books except over lunch, and every book looks like a bestseller after two Camparis and soda. I once had a lunch with a publisher which was so monumental he rang me up next day to ask what was the book we had been talking about.

But this doesn't mean a COP will avoid a business lunch. It's the business that's avoided, not the lunch. There's no need to pass up a free meal. Simply say it is a company rule never to discuss business in public, for security reasons (some com-

It's the business that's avoided . . .

panies really do have such a rule). One may then relax and enjoy the food and drink, together with the other advantage of a working lunch: 'It's not worth going back to the office now.'

Private Hospital Treatment

Health insurance as a perk can be two-edged. An employee who has to go into a public hospital is at least assured of a rest from work. Nobody from the office is anxious to visit those dreadful long Nightingale wards full of groaning people, and those that do get out as quickly as possible. The worker cannot be contacted on the phone and at any minute is liable to be loaded onto a trolley and wheeled off to another ward. The main impression in most hospitals is that you have been cut off from society for ever.

But private hospitals have bedside phones and rooms like hotel suites. The patient receives a stream of visitors, many of them senior colleagues who bring 'just a few reports you might like to look over as you're doing nothing' (nothing, the patient thinks, except clutch my stomach and groan). Sometimes the office will phone the sick employee, to ask how he is and tell him they're sending along the monthly sales report to cheer him up.

Recently I visited a pal in a private hospital and he was sitting in his luxurious suite looking completely miserable. 'I am a ruined man,' he told me.

'You mean the cost of the operation?'

'No, that's covered. It's the cost of entertaining my friends. I have to pay that myself. Once they discovered I can have unlimited drink and food served in my room they've been flocking here in droves. You just press a bell and they bring it. They've even got a wine nurse. The area sales manager has been to lunch three times. He says it's the best claret he's ever tasted. Today they sent me a bill for the first week – £47 for wines, spirits and guest meals.'

111

The phone rang. 'Yes,' he said into it, 'I would love it if you sent over details of the new reorganization scheme. Thank you, it only hurts when I laugh.'

8

The Social Side

For when the wine is in, the wit is out.
Thomas Becon

Office social life can be more important than any aspect of the job. I write as one who saw a girl who'd left for another firm lured back at enormous expense because she used to bring in home-made cakes for tea every afternoon and was also active as an amateur sex therapist.

When a person is made redundant in April, how many realize it is because of the office party in December? Office parties are the most dangerous events of the commercial year. Think back. Did you lurch up to the personnel manager and say, 'The trouble with you, old chap, is that you haven't ever had any practical experience'? Did you tell the sales manager he didn't know what he was talking about? If so, shudder. Don't fool yourself they were too sozzled to remember. One thing that distinguishes senior management from ordinary mortals is that they *always* remember anything nasty, no matter how much they had to drink. (It is, by the way, equally astonishing how they forget nice things. Lend them a fountain pen and it will never be seen again. But they remember foul, evil-smelling situations perfectly.)

Flattery is as bad as rudeness. It is lethal to put an arm round the departmental chief and say, 'I want you to know, old man, that I think you're the greatest little boss in all the world and I

113

really do mean that most sincerely . . . .' You might as well punch him on the nose.

So complicated are the politics of the office party it's posible to commit a terrible offence without knowing it. I shall never forget some years ago getting into trouble over something at the Christmas party *which I couldn't remember*. When I went back after the holidays everyone looked at me in a strange manner and giggled.

Usually after something like that there's a clue – lipstick on the collar, mud on the trousers or a crushed sandwich in the pocket. But this time, nothing. True, there were odd blank moments – you don't drink three bottles of cheap EEC hock without the brain being affected a trifle – but no hint as to what had happened except the fact that a fortnight later I was transferred.

The trouble is, of course, that under the influence of alcohol the partygoer is liable to think he's doing everyone a favour. I once watched with horror as a sixteen-year-old messenger danced with the chairman's wife on an office riverboat shuffle down the Thames, covering her expensive white dress in grubby fingermarks. Sometimes a wife is only too pleased to be danced with, and that is equally fraught. Askew claims that when he seduced the chief accountant's wife in his own office one Christmas he really thought he was not only doing her a favour, but he was doing the accountant a favour too, as according to his wife he had lost interest in sex years previously. The accountant disagreed and Askew's own leaving party was held shortly afterwards.

There are certain rules which can alleviate the disastrous results of an office party. First, lock your own room unless you want someone to read all the files, to be sick all over it or make love in it. The same rules apply to a desk. A person is blamed for what happens in their room, whether they did it or not. If a man is found in a peculiar position with a girl in an office, it's the owner of the room who gets blamed, not the happy couple.

This is Law 31 of Coarse Office Life (Commercial Guilt Transference).

Leave any wooing (male or female) until afterwards. It is best to make an assignation in the pub round the corner. Then no jealousies are aroused.

Keep conversation with those senior to yourself away from business and sex. Try to find a neutral topic such as football or television.

Do not be absent from the room longer than necessary. People get suspicious. ('Where's old Joe? I bet he's up to some mischief . . . .')

If you find a senior executive in the cupboard with one of his female staff simply say, 'I'm sorry, I thought it was the lift', and leave.

Remember Law 35 of Coarse Office Life: A business executive is never off-duty. This also applies to senior civil servants, Treasury officials, admirals, headmasters, vice-chancellors, editors and politicians.

Social Events

Be seen to support social events, but do not become involved in organizing them. There is nothing more potent for stirring up strife. Office people, including bosses, don't remember great events such as the takeover or the great unemployment; they recall little things, like the time the central heating burst. For instance, the head office of a bank in London was thrown into chaos over icecream. They used to send out for it every afternoon in summer and one day there was a row over whose turn it was to fetch it. It ended with people taking sides and screaming at each other all over the building. When it was finally collected, a melting portion was placed in somebody's out tray and there was a fight with staff throwing icecream at each other. It is still remembered as The Great Choc Ice

Scandal. Since most social events are associated with disaster it does little for a COP to be in charge. Make a modest contribution in one definite area ('Daphne James kindly volunteered to do the flowers – aren't they nice?') and then keep well in the background.

My own lack of success in office life is largely due to ignoring this advice. Being a sociable sort of chap I was always trying to organize things and merely getting abused for my trouble.

The most dramatic failure was a coach outing to Brighton. For once I thought my luck was in, because everything went smoothly from the crates of lager on the way down to more lager on the way back. In fact trouble did not strike until the outskirts of London, when it was discovered that the cost accountant, a genial chap of about sixty, was trying to lick a receptionist's left breast. Needless to say, he was completely drunk. By the time the journey finished in Knightsbridge he was incapable of getting out of the coach and I, fool that I was, thought to gain credit by taking him home. A taxi was called and the unfortunate accountant helped into it, accompanied by myself. When we reached his flat, however, he became obstreperous and got out the wrong side of the taxi and stood in the middle of the Fulham Road waving his arms. And then, dear Lord, his trousers fell down so he stood there shouting in his underpants, with buses swerving all round him, while I tried to persuade him to move and pay the taxi driver at the same time.

A wiser man would have left him to be knocked down by a bus, but like an idiot I steered him to the front door and rang the bell. The door was opened by his wife, who had apparently seen his antics from the window and gave me a stream of abuse. Next day the managing director said he'd received a complaint from the accountant's wife that I'd got him drunk on the trip and was dancing about the middle of Fulham Road with him stripped naked. My defence was utterly useless. He hardly listened.

'You know he's diabetic, I suppose?' was the only reply.

'He'll probably be away for a week. Really, this sort of thing is too bad. Why are you always stirring up trouble like this?'

So much for my hard work on the coach trip. They never even paid for the taxi.

Do not think that by making a sycophantic speech at some function you can impress management. No speech has ever been written that didn't offend somebody, if only because their name was left out. My worst effort in this respect was at a sales conference where they asked me to speak with the idea of providing a light interlude before the droning monotony of the marketing director's address. I was known in the organization as something of a comedian and there was a buzz of anticipation as I rose. Indeed, all might have been well but for the fact that just before I spoke they asked me to announce that a veteran member of the company had died that afternoon.

I stood up and asked for silence, a request that was greeted with hoots of merriment. I said: Please could we have some quiet, as I have a serious announcement to make (more mirth and shouts of 'This had better be good').

'No, no, really,' I protested, 'this is not funny gentlemen.' (*Collapse of half a dozen people*). 'As we all know, poor old Syd Nicholas has been in failing health for some time.' (*Cries of 'Yes, the old bastard got VD in the Boer War'*.) 'No, please, this is no joking matter.' (*Another explosion of jollity.*) 'I am being serious.' (*A voice: 'First time in your life then'*.) 'It is with deep regret I have to announce that Syd Nicholas passed peacefully away in hospital this afternoon.' (*Complete collapse of whole assembly, mingled with shouts of, 'That's the unfunniest joke I ever heard' and 'When's the pay-off coming, then?'*)

Later, in the toilets, I heard two highly placed executives saying it was absolutely disgraceful to make a speech like that, what a terrible thing to try to make a joke out of poor old Syd's death, if the chap had any decency he'd resign immediately. A pretty rotten reward for spending two nights writing a speech. The only person who got anything out of it seemed to be Syd. At least he didn't pass to that Greater Territory in the Sky (as the marketing director happily phrased it) without recognition.

Sporting events are as lethal as social occasions, and once again a COP must avoid becoming involved except as a spectator. I shall never forget rashly taking part in the annual cricket match between head office in London and the works in South Wales, and running out the chairman for nought. It was not entirely my fault, as he was so dazed with his lunchtime gin that he didn't hear my call and stood there swaying while I thundered down the pitch. A succession of fresh batsmen brought grim news as I batted on. 'Sir Sydney is very upset about what you did,' muttered the next man, and the one after him hissed, 'Sir Sydney says he wants to see you when you are out.' I have never batted better in my life; to delay the interview I played like a Test cricketer. But in the end I had to come in and there was Sir Sydney blubbering into a great tankard of gin and snarling, 'That was the worst thing anyone has ever done to me on the cricket field.'

Sir Sydney had his reward, because when we fielded they put him on to bowl. All the middle and senior management batsmen immediately gave themselves up with sycophantic cries of 'Jolly well bowled, sir. I didn't know what that ball was doing' (neither did Sir Sydney). Players from the foundry, however, took great pleasure in clouting him all over the field.

One of the problems of office sport is that people who want to keep well in with management won't play properly. At soccer they stand back from the ball so a senior man can have a shot, and the goalkeeper will probably lie down to let the ball through. Meanwhile works employees, perhaps threatened with redundancy, rejoice in the chance of kicking hell out of a senior man.

The last word in office sport is to partner a senior executive in a golf match. When I was in the PR department of an industrial firm they asked me to partner a visiting vice-president of the American parent company in a foursome. I got the job not because of any positive qualities, but because everyone else was scared stiff of committing some dreadful blunder. He seemed a pleasant old chap and I thought I might get away with it. But I am not the best of golfers and, being unusually nervous, I began by sending my drive straight into the forehead of the finance director, who was standing to one side of the first tee about thirty yards away. With a terrible cry he collapsed unconscious. Unfortunately he fell on top of the ball. Thinking to ingratiate myself with my important partner, I asked them to roll him over so that the vice-president could play his shot from where the ball lay, according to the rules of golf. My simple suggestion was greeted with a ghastly silence and the elderly American was horrified. 'Gee, that poor guy,' he kept muttering all the way round the course, as we went from disaster to disaster. I think it was at that moment a process started which ended six months later when they told me they were economizing and I would have to go. By then the injured man had recovered, but he had a peculiar aversion to me and if he saw me in the corridor he would go white, clench his teeth and walk rapidly in the opposite direction.

Sex in the Office

The utmost care is needed in conducting an emotional affair in the office. Romances between ordinary employees can be conducted freely, and may even be encouraged, in the way slaves were encouraged to breed in the old plantations of the American Southern States. But among higher ranks there is a strict pecking order. Men should never have an affair with the secretary of someone above them in the hierarchy. One international detergent manufacturer has a strict rule that staff are only allowed to seduce their own secretaries; it is absolutely forbidden to have an affair with someone else's secretary.

Women must show equal caution. While, to some extent,

they are protected by the old-fashioned idea that an affair must be the man's responsibility, they may still be blamed. If an executive's secretary has an affair with someone lower down, then the executive himself feels lowered. I knew one director who was so furious when his secretary started going out with a driver that he spoke to her about it. 'It reflects on me,' he said. 'Why can't you go out with someone like Mr Johnson?' (Mr Johnson was the research director. It is true he was single, but only because he hated women.)

Discretion is vital. Many men have deep, hidden desires. We once had a middle-aged tealady with whom I used to flirt, and one Christmas Eve I put my arm round her when she wheeled round the trolley. The departmental head, a bald-headed little man of about fifty-five with bulging eyes, turned on me with a look of pure jealousy and hatred. It was frightening, those eyes staring at me from behind rimless spectacles. Apparently he had fancied the tealady for years but was afraid to do anything about it.

Women have special problems, the chief of which is sexual harassment, to use the current phrase – although I must say, in passing, that this is a little hard on men. If no man ever harassed a girl the human race would die out. As Uncle Walter used to say: 'My boy, unless I had got the courage to kiss your aunt under the mistletoe in the stationery store, you would never have had any cousins.' But as a rule the amount of genuine sex involved is in inverse ratio to the amount of harassment. The sort of man who is constantly patting women's bottoms is unlikely to go further. Probably he daren't. A good way to get rid of the persistent wolf may be to offer instant sex. My former girlfriend was so fed up with the office groper that she confronted him and said, 'Look, do you really want sex? Because if so, let's go into your office and have it.' He began to haver, and the more he havered the more insistent she was. In the end he made his excuses and left, to coin a phrase, and never pestered her again. But don't blame me if this wheeze misfires and you find you have offered yourself to the local sex maniac, a man of incredible potency and desire (someone like myself, in fact).

The cleverest counter-attack on sexual harassment I've encountered was made by a girl who became so tired of a colleague's advances she left a note in large letters on her desk: 'Gone to see doctor re herpes.'

An entanglement with someone senior can be risky for women. Many a girl has found that once she'd delivered the goods to her boss she was acting as unpaid general help as well as secretary and mistress. A girl I know had an affair with her boss, who had been divorced twice, and he invited her down to his country home for the weekend. She was looking forward to two days of romantic bliss, only to find that three children of his previous marriage were spending the weekend there and she was acting as nursemaid, babysitter, cook and washer-up. The last straw came when he tried to dictate a letter while lying in a deckchair in the garden. 'I suddenly asked myself why I was doing this,' she said.

Where to consummate an affair may be a problem. Never use the office. Perhaps it's punishment for sin, but Law 5 of Coarse Office Life says that upon a couple starting to make love in a deserted part of the building someone will enter. As a young man, my friend Askew had a terrible experience when he went into the basement with a girl colleague after closing time. Suddenly the place was flooded with light and an army of workmen marched in and started removing everything. They were politeness itself, although one did ask, 'Would you mind lying over there, guv'nor?', but to continue was impossible. Furthermore, the dreadful shock gave Askew a psychological disturbance, so that ever since he has not been able to make love except in bed.

Affairs at work are easier for senior staff because there's a private office. But the mere fact that a room is locked with a couple inside is enough to condemn them. Nobody will believe

The mere fact that a room is locked with a couple inside is enough to condemn them

it when you say, 'We were going through some important papers and didn't want to be disturbed.' As a general rule, let sex rear its ugly head only outside the premises.

A problem of relationships in the office is how to talk to one's partner the morning after consummation. In the past, if an executive slept with his secretary there was usually a good deal of outward coldness in the morning: 'Good morning, Mr Watson. I trust you had a good journey to town this morning, and that Mrs Watson is well?' (*Sotto voce*: 'You've got a stain on your trousers. Sponge it off.')

And the reply, 'Er – yes, Janice . . . I mean Miss Jackson . . . it was a most enjoyable journey. Would you please ring Interflora and send fifty pounds' worth of roses to my wife and say I'm sorry I was detained in London last night.'

Now there is the new difficulty of the female executive who may have been involved with a member of her staff. It is rather awkward if he is the brash sort who goes around leering and talking loudly about the previous night:'My, Janice, you look smashing this morning. Wouldn't think you'd been on the job all night. By the way, I left my watch on the bedside table.' It is not easy to cope with this, especially if you have to give him orders to do something menial. Anybody brash enough to behave like that will be totally insensitive to all hints, so it is best to use the bludgeon. Hiss quietly, 'Shut up, Charlie, or I won't give it you again and that is a promise.' If that has no effect, swear to tell everyone he was no good in bed. But this is a last resort.

Leaving Ceremonies

A regular ceremony in the office social calendar is the retirement or leaving party. These take two forms. The first is the official function. All are asked to gather in Mr Smethurst's office at 4.30 and the genial Mr Smethurst makes a speech about how much we all love Fred and how sorry we are that he is leaving (redundant after thirty years, but no one mentions that) and we would like to present him with a chiming clock on behalf of the firm. Furthermore his colleagues in the buying department have collected for an electric blanket which should warm the cockles of his heart if not his cockle itself (loud laughter) and would Fred like to say something? And Fred says he isn't used to speaking much but he would like to thank everyone for their lovely electric toaster – sorry, blanket – and especially Mr Smethurst and the firm for the clock and he knows his wife will be delighted too and he hopes to call in and see them all frequently. Then comes the big surprise – genial, plump Mrs Wallace of the canteen wheels in three bottles of Cyprus sherry and everyone has a genial, plump glass after which Mr Smethurst, thankful he doesn't have to live on Fred's pension, hurries away as quickly as possible as the A40 gets very crowded after five o'clock.

The unofficial retirement function is different. The normal routine is for the happy leaver to adjourn to the nearest pub at Friday lunchtime and hold court for colleagues until closing time. It is advisable to arrive early, as latecomers may find themselves buying a round for thirty-five people, some of whom don't even work at the office. Alternatively, the party may be in the office, with a dozen litre bottles of cheap Spanish plonk and one bag of crisps among forty people. The amount of booze flowing can arouse deep emotions. The atmosphere of a leaving 'do' is highly charged and it only needs a spark for things to get out of hand.

A little sentimentality is to be expected, of course, so don't pay any attention when the leaver drunkenly says you were the only decent person in the whole shebang or confesses a dreadful secret, such as the fact he has been living off the tea money for six months or sleeping with the lady who comes to clean the telephones. Ignore the invariable offer to fix up friends with a job at his new place (he won't want to know on Monday).

The retirement or leaving party

These are harmless fantasies. What has to be feared is when the ugly spirit of rebellion rears its head, especially if the leaver is not going of his own free will.

In this case the aggrieved person will probably spend most of the party telling everyone what he is going to do to the boss before he departs, and then failing to do it. I remember a man who said he would go into the boss's office, spit on his desk and then march out again in total silence. We spent the whole lunch hour trying to persuade him against this foolish deed. 'Don't do it, Charlie. Don't go into Mr Johnson's room and spit all over him – you'll never get another job, they'll stop your cheque, etc. etc.' He left the pub waving his arms and issuing threats, and actually marched into the chief's room sucking a sweet to get a lot of spit. According to the executive's secretary, who happened to be there, he then breathed beer fumes over the room, mumbled something about having come to say goodbye, and left. Charlie's story, which became an office legend, was a wild yarn in which the cringing executive was pursued round his office by a shower of saliva. Such is human nature, Charlie's version was believed.

The danger of merry japes is that innocent people become involved. Which is why the wise person quits before the party ends, as I should have done when the man who was leaving led a party of us back to the office where we sang 'The Red Flag' outside the managing director's office. As the last line died away he opened his door. I turned to flee and found I was the only person left – the others had ratted and could be heard scuttling back to safety down the corridor. It is not easy to explain to a managing director why you have been singing 'The Red Flag' outside his office and I did not attempt to try. Later that afternoon the office humorist pasted up a large copy of the main points from the Sermon on the Mount on the door, with the bits about the meek inheriting the earth underlined. It was obvious I would be blamed, and I was trying to scrape it off when the noise attracted his attention and for the second time that day he opened his door to find me standing there, this time holding a knife and covered in bits of paper. I merely mention these unpleasant incidents to illustrate the importance of getting away early and not becoming involved.

This particularly applies if the leaver spends the afternoon lurching drunkenly round the office saying goodbye and trying to grope the girls. It will do no good to be seen supporting him in the corridor or holding his head under a tap. Treat anyone who throws a leaving party as a leper once the party is over.

9

Quitting the Job and Retirement

It is not fit you should sit here any longer . . . you shall now give
place to better men.
Oliver Cromwell

There are many reasons for leaving a job: resignation; another
post; redundancy; the sack; retirement; ill health; pregnancy;
and death. A COP who is single should take precautions
against death. It may be impossible to stop dying, but at least
make sure you aren't buried by the firm. One of my many
employers buried the switchboard lady when she died, as she
was single and had no relatives, and it was a terrible funeral.
One miserable wreath and only two mourners – me and the
boss, who kept his hat on all the time in church, as he had never
been in one before. They argued for months about who should
pay and whether they could deduct the cost from her pension
contributions. The boss got drunk afterwards and charged it to
the firm. I always think that the ultimate horror for an author
must be to be buried by his publishers.

Voluntary resignation is, of course, the easiest and most
comfortable form of departure. The important thing is not to
give way to a temptation to get your revenge. Askew, for
instance, spent ten minutes abusing his boss when he resigned.
The abuse was received with a thin smile and the information
that Askew's new firm was a subsidiary of the organization. 'So
we shall still be able to see each other,' said the boss grimly. 'I
might even get transferred there later.' Askew's efforts to make

128

I always think that the ultimate horror for an author must be to be buried by his publishers

amends ('There's a speck of dust on your coat, sir, let me dust it off') were unavailing and his career with the new firm short.

If the desire for revenge is overwhelming, be discreet. Do no more than hint at dark goings on in the letter of resignation: 'In conclusion I should like to state how happy I have been here. Indeed, the only jarring note has been that I could never accept the common practice of making unrestricted private phone calls, many of them long-distance, on the company lines . . . .' Or perhaps one might hint at obstruction by senior staff: 'My decision, I must admit, has been influenced by the fact that I have been passed over for promotion twice/not had a new car for three years/been given a desk near the door, etc. etc.' Go no further. You never know when you might need people.

The Sack

Few people are actually dismissed these days, so under this heading I include any manner of forced departure such as compulsory redundancy or retirement. They are all the sack under different names – only the conditions may be different. Some sting has been taken out of dismissal in recent years by legislation, so the drama of instant sacking with raised voices and shaking finger pointed at the door is less frequent. Even so it is still heard. And, of course, there are always self-employed and part-time people without legal protection, while some employers seem to regard anyone who is defenceless (for example, middle-aged divorced women with children and no alimony) as outside the law.

One must still shed a tear for the Great Sackings of old. In particular I recall one in the Midlands. The firm was small and mean and the owner had a fixation about people who leaned back in their chairs and broke them. Time after time he warned a huge lout of nineteen what would happen if he broke his chair. Well, one day he leaned back and he did break it. We looked

130

desperately for somewhere to hide it. Then we heard the boss coming and in panic threw it out of the window into a large tree which grew behind the office. The leaves covered it completely and we shuffled round all the other chairs to disguise the fact that one was missing.

Come the autumn . . . the leaves fell, revealing the chair still in the tree in all its glory. We lived on the edge of a volcano for ten days and then the boss (whose office faced the other direction) came into our room and, glancing through the window, saw the chair perched in the bare branches. The effect was dramatic. He pointed a trembling finger at the door and shouted, 'You wretched boy, get out of here at once!' The culprit slunk from the room and we collapsed in helpless laughter while the employer gibbered and foamed with rage. He actually did gibber.

Most sackings today are less spectacular, and sometimes it is impossible for an employee to tell if he or she is being fired. I knew one chap who was called in to see the departmental head who hummed and hahed and said what a good fellow he had been and how sorry they would be to lose him, with the result he came out believing he was going to be promoted. The conversation apparently began with the executive praising my friend's work and then saying, 'I can't say how much we shall miss you when you have gone.'

'That's very decent of you,' said my friend, 'but I'm not going anywhere.'

'Of course not,' came the reply. 'You are not going *any*where. You are going *some*where. You are a man with ambition. Frank, I congratulate you. Good luck in your future career. You are on the verge of big things.' With which he shook him warmly by the hand.

The truth only dawned on Friday when he found three months' wages in his packet. 'That's funny,' he said, 'they've also returned all my pension contributions for some reason. I shall have to see the boss about this.'

131

Since the last person to know they're going is always the person who's leaving, study the signs. The following phrases, used by cowardly bosses to disguise their real meaning, all mean the same thing.

I am worried about your future here.
Have you ever thought of moving?
Do you want to stay in this job all your life?
You're not really happy here, are you?
Have you ever considered doing something else?
What would you say to the chance to make a fresh start?
We feel we are standing in the way of your career.
We don't want to keep you against your better interests.
We can never give you the chance you deserve.

I see no reason why anybody should make it easier for the man who is spouting this rubbish. Reply, 'No, I am quite happy here. I have never considered moving. I don't want to make a fresh start. You give me all the chances I want.' This will considerably embarrass the boss, because you are supposed to play the game and cooperate by saying, 'Well, now you mention it, I *had* thought of moving on . . . .' Make the man say what he means.

Other signs of impending departure which may be overlooked or misinterpreted are:

Everybody is suddenly nice to you.
Expenses are not queried.
Senior staff start agreeing.
A newspaper open at Situations Vacant is left on the desk.
People draw your attention to other jobs.
The commissionaire stops joking with you.

Nobody will discuss the future. It's as if you've got an incurable disease. Ask them what they are doing for Christmas and they blush and look away in embarrassment as if to say, 'What the hell are you interested in Christmas for, you're not going to be here.' Your name is omitted from future events such as the annual sports day or the Derby sweepstake.

Many an office worker has first discovered his dismissal when he finds a list pinned on the wall asking for contributions to his farewell gift. So keep an eye open for news of any collection.

When the blow falls, don't waste time grovelling and snivelling about what a shock this has been. It will make no difference. The decision has been made, and probably not by the person who's delivering the message. I always remember calling regularly on a Midlands firm with two nice receptionists. One day both of them were missing and I mentioned it to the production director, who said, 'Oh, yes, we needed to economize so we sacked one of the receptionists.'

'Which one?' I asked, and he replied, 'The fat one.'

When you're just 'the fat one' to an organization there's not much use snivelling about being dismissed. But by all means make the person doing the dirty work feel a heel. Abuse is useless – it merely makes the sacker feel he is justified. Hurt dignity is best. 'I must say, Philip, I am rather surprised at this after what you said when I drove you home from the office party. If I remember rightly your exact words then were, "Goodnight, old chap, I'll never forget your kindness in taking me home when I'm drunk." ' Readers can doubtless make up their own replies.

Among the worst people for handing out dismissal are those who profess political or religious views of a liberal nature. I once worked for someone who had formerly been the union branch secretary. He stood no nonsense from anybody, to quote his own words, which in practice meant he behaved like Hitler with a headache. Yet he was no worse than the religious maniac who sacked a girl and then told her, 'I shall pray for you.'

'And I shall pray for you,' said the girl. 'I shall ask Him to break your neck.'

Note that if you *want* the sack it's impossible to get it. Whatever the COP does he or she is kept on (Law 29). When I was in the army I used to pray for an ignominious discharge, but instead they promoted me.

Be careful of anticipating departure. Some people, believing they are on the way out, commit an act which means they've got to be fired anyway. I am thinking of a young man in a small advertising agency whose work as a designer was appalling. The two partners who ran the firm stuck it as long as they could and then held a conference. They began by deciding to sack the offender but realized neither had the heart to do so, so decided to let him stay and called the chap in to tell him the good news. Unfortunately, he knew he was being discussed and, fortified by half a bottle of scotch, he bounded up the stair with a cry of 'You stinking bastards!' and thundered into the partner's office where he bellowed, 'You bastards want to sack me, don't you? Well, you can't do that and get away with it.' The two partners rushed round him crying out that he wasn't going to be fired, they all loved him, but he paid no attention and, seizing a typewriter, threw it through the window. So then the partners started shouting that now he *was* going to be fired, but for a different reason.

If departure is not voluntary I see no reason why the COP should not leave a souvenir behind in the shape of some merry jest. A dismissed sales rep once sent a fictitious paragraph to the house magazine stating that the marketing director was getting married again and welcoming everybody to a champagne party in his office that Friday evening. Like most employees, the marketing director never read the magazine and was astonished to find himself besieged by 200 thirsty people that Friday, including the company chairman who boomed, 'A splendid gesture, Frank, open-hearted and generous and typical of you. Sorry to hear about you and Jane splitting up, though.' Among the guests were the editor of the house magazine with a photographer, and one or two senior staff who had collected for a silver salver. The outraged executive pinned a notice on his door saying PARTY CAN-CELLED and fled, only to find someone had posted the magazine to his wife at home, where the atmosphere was unbearable for weeks.

Less subtle was the action of a man who upon his departure hid an evil-smelling dog turd in the air-conditioning louvres and received a desperate phone call three days later imploring him to tell them where it was.

If you have reason to suspect there will be no office presentation you are entitled to show displeasure. This is best done by telling everybody, 'Please don't collect any money for *me* – give it all to cancer research.' After that they can hardly fail to raise something, and a worthy cause will benefit. I invented this wheeze many years ago when I left the now defunct *Birmingham Gazette*. During three years there I'd contributed to ten leaving gifts (they went like flies in those days) and two marriage presents (both shotgun weddings – contraception was terrible in Birmingham in the fifties), yet when I came to go I saw no signs of a collection for myself. So I told the deputy editor to give my money to cancer research. He felt so ashamed he had no choice but to organize a collection.

If a presentation *is* made, exercise self-control during the ceremony. By some quirk of office life the presentation is usually made by the same person who has dished out the sack. To add insult to injury they have a habit of making a speech of praise, saying how hard you worked and how popular you were, and how you can never be replaced. Restrain any desire to shout, 'Why the hell are you getting rid of me, then?' Do not attempt to pay off any old scores in the reply. As at any execution, the victim is expected to forgive.

Owing to the difficulties of directly dismissing an employee, more employers are instead making life so unpleasant that they leave voluntarily, a process known as 'sickening'. Not that it is anything new. Quite early in my career I saw an elderly

135

assistant editor, who refused to give up his post, removed by the simple process of taking away his desk. There was quite literally nowhere for him to go. He used to wander around the office trying to sit down and being asked to move. Eventually he took refuge in the office library and in the end took the hint and left.

A common way of sickening employees is to post them somewhere unpleasant. I once stoped at a hotel in Scunthorpe and found the whole place full of businessmen who were being pressured into resigning. People were asking each other, 'What did you do wrong?' It was like sleeping in an elephants' graveyard. The unpleasant place need not be outside the office. When I worked in public relations they had a man with bad asthma who was given a desk in an attic at the top of the building. They knew he couldn't face the stairs.

Jobs which involve foreign postings offer the biggest opportunities for discipline by exile. I suppose the Foreign Office must be the greatest exponent of the art of sickening, but some commercial organizations come pretty close.

'Ah, come in, Frogworthy. You will be pleased to hear we are sending you to Gomboland.'

'I wouldn't have thought there would have been much scope for toilet products there, sir.'

'There isn't. You will create the demand, Frogworthy.'

'Can I take the family?'

'It wouldn't be advisable. Your wife would not like the climate, and if the children left the house they might get eaten.'

'By tigers?'

'No, by local residents. Off you go, Frogworthy.'

'Au revoir, sir.'

'Not au revoir, Frogworthy. Goodbye.'

Another form of persuasion is to give the person in question an impossible task, such as stamping out immorality in the typing pool. My old Uncle Walter claims he was once told to double the sales of the company's worst product. A favourite wheeze used to be posting the victim to some saleman's graveyard in the far North of Scotland with instructions to sell something inappropriate, such as suntan lotion.

There is an American company which, when it wishes to fire a middle-range executive, makes him personal assistant to the company president. At the last count he had fourteen personal assistants. There are no duties, but the holders are made to carry the blame for everything that goes wrong. 'It's like Death Row,' said my informant. 'Every so often one of them just disappears.'

'Special Projects' is a favourite Btitish venue for those On the Way Out. Many an executive is heard to cry : 'My God, not Special Projects' as he opens his mail.

A new form of dismissal today is to invite people to leave and rejoin on a self-employed basis. At first this looks irresistible, since the money offered is probably a little more than staff pay. Besides, everyone wants to be their own boss. But before jumping in, ask why they are doing it. It is because they are going to save enormous sums on national insurance, pensions, holiday pay, sick pay and other overheads. Most important of all, part-timers and self-employed people are easier to sack. In the cuts in local government and education of recent years, hardly any full-time employees were dismissed. Part-timers such as music teachers and dinner ladies bore the brunt.

I was once fired from a part-time job by the receptionist. I used to help edit this firm's house magazine, and one day when I arrived for my monthly stint the receptionist said, 'Do you want anything, Mr Green?' and I said, yes, I'd come in as usual to help with the magazine, and she said, 'Oh, they asked me to tell you they won't need you any more.' She added hastily, 'You can't see them, they're all out.' Being a freelance I had no redress except to kick the door of the lift. The dent must still be there.

The worst problem of self-employed life is getting money out of people. Only last year a group of theiving scoundrels in

Germany, calling themselves publishers, refused to pay £1,000 they owed me with the calm statement, 'Times are difficult for publishers now in Germany. We are rather poor at the moment.' My agent replied, 'Times are also difficult for authors in England. We, too, are rather poor.' They replied to this by going bankrupt.

Working for yourself makes you bitter and twisted. Suddenly you realize the pension rights of a quite junior employed person are worth £100,000 and much more in the public service. Eventually you hate everyone. I was recently drinking with a pal who ran his own struggling business, when he suddenly turned pale and breathed heavily. I asked what the matter was and he told me, 'That man opposite has just retired at fifty-five, and his pension is twice what I earned last year.'

Early Retirement

The best method of leaving is to take early retirement on favourable terms (retirement on bad terms is worse than the sack). Unfortunately, that isn't always possible except in some areas of the public sector, such as local government or the BBC, where staff are retired on full pension at the taxpayers' expense, at an age when most people are wondering what to do when they grow up. However, it is possible to encourage early departure.

It is not as easy as it might seem. Pouring a bucketful of fertilizer over the head of a senior executive may earn dismissal with a frozen pension rather than retirement; so may destroying your desk with a hatchet. On the other hand, idleness and inefficiency will not help either. They may even earn promotion. I knew one man who stopped working in an effort to force the firm's hand. The less he did, the more they promoted him. Despite the fact that he had a couch moved into his office he was still soldiering on well into his sixties. The fact is, once those at the top suspect an employee is angling for early retirement they try to obstruct them. They too would like to leave prematurely, and they have nothing to gain from your departure since they are senior.

The employee who fails is one who from the age of forty-five puts a large calendar on his desk and starts crossing off the days; who keeps saying, 'Of course, I'm hoping for early retirement; I don't intend to stay here until I'm sixty-five.' Such people are usually kept on the hook and released grudgingly.

So keep up the pretence of enthusiasm until the last moment. Make projections well into the future. Then, when the hour comes, strike. The most dramatic action I recall was that of a man of fifty-eight who had a sex change operation and claimed that as a woman he could retire at sixty. More effective was the wheeze of a civil servant who simply arrived one day with a kipper nailed to his bowler hat. He took it off, hung it on the coat rack and sat down as if nothing had happened. In the end he wore them down. 'You can't entrust important government secrets to a man with a kipper nailed to his hat,' said the divisional head with some force, 'especially when he denies it's there.'

But action must be *sudden*. It is useless to fade into ill health, groaning as you go up the stairs and panting, 'I'm too old for this job, I ought to have early retirement.' People get used to gradual things. They'll say, 'Oh, he's been complaining about those stairs for years. There's nothing really wrong with him.' The essence of wangling an early pension is to select a sudden trauma in life and work on it. Ensure there is a watershed after which they will say, 'He was never the same after . . . .' Examples to fill in the missing words are: his operation; he fell off his bicycle; his wife left him; his son became a hippie; his car crash; the time he stuck a fork through his foot while gardening and pinned himself to the lawn.

I once had a colleague of about fifty-five whose wife deserted

139

him. For months afterwards he used to keep a photograph of her on his desk, look at it and sigh and kiss it; sometimes he even sobbed over it. It was too much for everybody and he duly left with the epitaph, 'He was never the same after his wife left.' We discovered later that as soon as his wife went he had taken up with a twenty-two-year-old secretary in another firm and was living with her all the time he was moaning about how lonely he was. After retiring he had the cheek to bring his lovely paramour into the office and parade her round, showing off the fact she was now heavily pregnant.

An operation is a wonderful chance. Most men and women over fifty need one, whether it's a hernia, a vasectomy or varicose veins. If nature should cooperate by offering an operation, remember the Golden Wheeze: Never recover. 'He was never the same after his operation' is the epitaph of many a fit, smiling pensioner, playing golf or tending the roses. Very little falsification is required. An operation leaves the patient feeling pretty terrible anyway. Just fail to improve, and move around the office clutching your gut and groaning occasionally, as you did in hospital.

The most magnificent wheeze of this kind was employed by a colleague whose trauma was a car crash. Whether the accident was real or not we shall never know, but he claimed the shock gave him nervous asthma. It could come on at any time, especially when people were being nasty or when he had to make a difficult decision. He would start to wheeze and groan and drag out an oxygen device and thrust it over his face so people couldn't speak to him. Every time the discussion came round to him at a conference he would put the mask on and answer by signs.

Then came the Master Wheeze. He said he couldn't stand cigarette smoke or dust, which meant he could hardly go anywhere in the building except his own office. Finally he took to carrying about a portable spittoon for use when attacks came on. These would culminate in a fit of coughing in the middle of

'He was never the same after his operation'

which he would produce his cuspidor, use it, close the lid, and *place it back on the table*. It was labelled in large letters

PHLEGM BOX

He left this all over the office. 'I don't suppose you've seen a box of phlegm anywhere, have you?' he used to ask. 'I must have lost it. Perhaps I left it in the canteen.'

As may be imagined, he got early retirement rapidly and wrote a long letter of thanks for the electric clock and said we would be pleased to hear that since he had stopped work his chest was much better. Three months later he was found to be working for another firm.

That seems an appropriate place to leave the world of the Coarse Office. But a final word of advice: Never return. There is no sadder sight than the former employee coming back to see his old pals and being asked by a new receptionist, 'Did you want something?' Besides, as soon as one leaves they always seem to double everybody's salary and promote all your old colleagues, and you feel jealous. The new people they hire are all incredibly young and the whole place suddenly becomes very unfamiliar.

There are other hazards, too. When my friend Askew returned to his office to jeer at former colleagues he was buttonholed in the corridor by the accountant who said, 'Just the man we want to see. The auditors are querying some of your expense sheets.'

After retirement my Uncle Walter was always returning to the old firm, ostensibly to see former pals but in reality to get a cheap lunch at the canteen followed by a subsidized pint of beer at the social club. After lunch he would sit on people's desks, breathing beer fumes all over the office, and loudly tell new-comers how to swindle the firm, while everybody cringed in embarrassment. In the end they asked him to cut out his visits as he was corrupting younger members of staff.

CENTURY HUTCHINSON
LIMITED

Inter-Office Memo

From: Editorial Director
        . . . .

To: Joanne
        . . . .

    If Michael Green rings up with any more piffling alterations to his book, tell him I'm in conference and will be there all day.